Gourmet
BARBECUE
C·O·O·K·E·R·Y

Gourmet BARBECUE C·O·O·K·E·R·Y

CHARMAINE SOLOMON

Illustrations by Toula Antonakos

GRUB STREET · LONDON

Published by
Grub Street
Golden House
28–31 Great Pulteney St
London W1

First impression in hardback 1986
Copyright © 1986 Grub Street, London
Text copyright © Charmaine Solomon
Design copyright © Grub Street, London

Photographs by Julie Fisher

British Library Cataloguing in Publication
Data

Solomon, Charmaine
    Gourmet barbecue cooking.
    1. Barbecue cookery
    I. Title
    641.7′6   TX840.B3

    ISBN 0-948817-01-1

Computerset by Tradespools
Printed and bound in Italy by
New Interlitho

FOREWORD

The smallest barbecue I've cooked on was barely a few inches square. Dining tête à tête in the roof garden of the Singapore Hilton, we were served an appetizer of what Singapore is famous for – satays.

A mini-hibachi was brought to the table, and the skewers of spicily marinated meat placed on the grill over coals, so that we could enjoy them freshly cooked. With the satays came a wonderful peanut sauce. At the other end of the spectrum I recall a gala feast in Nuku'alofa, Tonga, in the beautiful South Pacific. It was for about a hundred guests and a great shallow pit had been prepared, in which many leaf-wrapped foods were steaming over stones at white heat. On a spit nearby a whole pig was being roasted over glowing coals, and when we ate, it was on waxy 'plates' provided by Nature with remarkable foresight, lengths of banana tree trunks which are formed in layers and separate into ideal moisture proof containers.

In between are many memories of other meals cooked over the coals, simple family outings . . . parties in the garden . . . a winter experience in France where the chef performed delicious miracles, standing before the impressive fireplace which was the focal point of the restaurant.

What is it that makes such a meal special? There is something so comforting about a fire, the red glow of coals, the smell of juices vaporising, the look of food as it gets that rich brown colour.

No one, but no one could ever suffer from loss of appetite at a barbecue, a statement borne out by people's willingness to attack even the pathetically charred chop or sausage, which are terribly common with the beginner barbecues. Not that they are to blame, if they haven't been helped along with a few rules to follow, how are they to know that cooking over the coals is a vastly different procedure from cooking in a kitchen.

I hope, in this book, to spell out a few do's and don'ts to help avoid common problems and then go on to the exciting part . . . recipes that are well within the scope of the interested amateur, and that enable one to experience the foods of different countries without going further than the patio or garden.

Happy barbecuing!

AT A GLANCE
MENU PLANNER

STARTERS

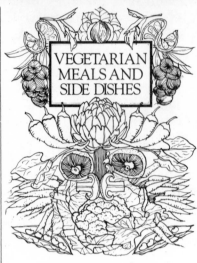

VEGETARIAN MEALS AND SIDE DISHES

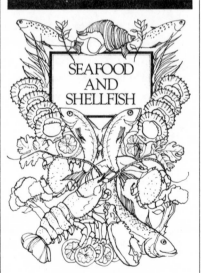

SEAFOOD AND SHELLFISH

Tuna Teriyaki 43

Coconut Fish Indochine 44

Curry-style Fish Kebabs 44

Goanese Fish with Green Herbs and Coconut 49

John Dory and Mange Tout en Papillote 49

Mexican Fish Steaks 50

Samaka Harrah 50

Stuffed Sardines in Vine Leaves 51

Korean Grillade 51

Grilled Trout with Spring Onions and Ginger 52

Otak Otak 52

Whole Fish with Ginger Soy Baste 53

Barbecued Fish with Taratoor Sauce 53

Snapper with Ginger Lemon Butter 54

Fish with Bacon and Tomato Sauce 54

POULTRY AND GAME

Almond Chicken Cardamom 56

Spatchcock with Orange Marinate and Hazelnut Stuffing 57

Honey Soy Chicken Wings 58

Barbecued Saffron Chicken 58

Tangerine Smoked Chicken 59

Pacific Island Picnic Parcels 60

Mango Chicken with Champagne 61

Tandoori-style Chilli Chicken 61

Thai Garlic Chicken 62

Chicken Satay 62

Tori Teriyaki 62

Tarragon Poussins with Gourmet Mushroom Sauce 64

Herbed Chicken with Walnut Sauce 69

Tandoori-style Chicken Kebabs 70

Chicken Pozharski 70

Oriental Barbecued Duckling 71

Indonesian Spiced Quail 72

Rajasthani-style Quail 72

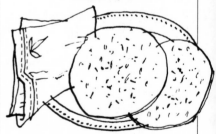

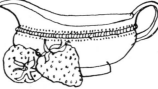
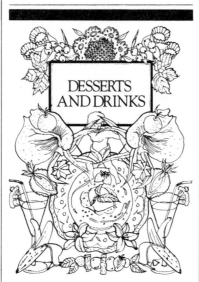

ENTERTAINING

Barbecues are a great way to entertain. Not only is there room for a gathering of any size, but there is the exhilaration of the open air setting, be it garden or woodland, the comfort of the crackling fire and the tantalizing smell of food sizzling on the grill.

In this book I have tried to provide recipes for all tastes and all occasions whether it is a special dish of quail, an exotic Eastern dish or something more suited for teenagers, such as hamburgers and salads which they can assemble on their own.

Choose your menu for the kind of party you are planning. When you shop for the barbecue, take into consideration the kind of cooking you intend to do, how many people you cook for, and where you will be cooking – in your own garden, patio, balcony, or out in the countryside.

With a little planning, much of the meal can be prepared well in advance. Have your fish, poultry or meat basting in the marinade the day before, prepare your salad greens in the morning and assemble just before guests arrive, or have your starters prepared on a tray and cook those while putting the finishing touches to the main dish. The nicest thing about barbecues is the relaxed, informal atmosphere and if you, the cook, have done a little work beforehand you will be able to enjoy yourself also.

Knowing the vagaries of wind and weather, I would like to assure the eager but apprehensive barbecue chef that each and every recipe has been chosen for its adaptability to oven, grill or frying pan, so no plans for a barbecue need be thwarted by the weather.

CHOOSING A BARBECUE

From my own experience and talking to other outdoor cooking enthusiasts I know what is ideal for one person is quite unacceptable to another.

At the two extremes are those with a strong pioneering streak who insist on gathering sticks of wood and building an outdoor fire, scorning such things as a wind shield or fire-starters apart from matches; then there are those who feel they need to build the biggest and best gas or electric barbecue, complete with tiled surrounds and every conceivable gadget for lifting, turning, flipping or skewering the food. Neither one nor the other guarantees the food will be a success – that is up to the cook.

For a start, we used to barbecue in the garden over a very modest contraption that was nothing more than a few bricks forming three sides of a square, with an iron grill supported on it. We were young and broke and couldn't afford to buy a barbecue, so it was just as well that the previous owners of the house had left some bricks lying around the yard!

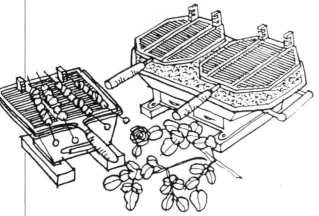

Our next step up was a *hibachi*, the Japanese name for a portable cast iron fire bowl with grates on the bottom and adjustable racks on top. This is compact and portable, even the triple bowl model fits easily in the back of a car. Briquets are the favoured fuel.

Later we graduated to a *kamado*, the Japanese earthenware stove cum smoke-oven cum cooker that features a double bowl with a hinged lid. The fire is controlled by means of a vent at the bottom and a damper top in the lid. A kamado is very heavy and therefore not for moving around, except from one side of a patio to the other on its metal cradle fitted with wheels.

Only charcoal is recommended for use in the kamado. It cooks with the lid either closed or open, but of course is much faster when heat is retained by closing the lid. The stout metal grill supplied with the kamado has bars that are too widely spaced for small pieces of food. I overcame the problem by placing a wire cake grid across the grill with the bars going the other way, so nothing falls through.

Faced with testing recipes for this book, I realised that building a fire of coals for each and every recipe was going to require more time than I had for the task. So I dashed out and invested in a gas barbecue and it has revolutionised barbecuing in our family.

It is not the most de luxe model, but it has burners which light at the touch of a button. No longer do I call on husband or son to get the fire going. Over the burners is a wire tray with volcanic rock. Now I cook over 'coals' that need only ten minutes to heat up, and there is no loss of flavour.

There are portable barbecues, table-top models, or others that come already built into a wagon with a very useful working surface on either side of the cooking area.

A portable barbecue can be as basic as a

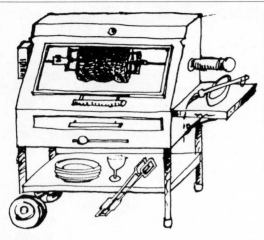

A griddle plate is the only practical way to cook hamburgers and other minced mixtures such as lentil patties or Pozharski cutlets. Sausages are best cooked on the griddle too, otherwise, the fat drips through the grill onto the fire and there is inevitably the kind of flare-up which should be avoided.

The plate is indispensable for griddle cakes or pancakes, but make sure the plate has been thoroughly cleaned or you may have a taste of hamburgers with your maple syrup.

When the griddle is not needed it is removed before starting the fire, and replaced with a third section of grill.

heavy metal bowl to hold the fire, covered with a wire grill on which to place the food. The grill should be capable of being raised or lowered, as this is the only way of controlling the amount of heat.

A kettle grill type of cooker with a hinged lid is useful, as the lid acts as a wind break so the barbecue can be turned to the position which provides the most protection. It can also be used as a covered cooker.

FIRST LIGHT YOUR FIRE

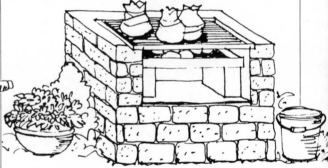

Whatever type of barbecue you choose, make sure it is built of sturdy material, and that it is stable. Metal should be heavy gauge with a finish that is able to withstand great heat. A well-designed model will have legs that cover at least as much area as the cooking top, and preferably have a shelf below on which the legs are braced. This is also useful for stacking plates and food.

The cooking area itself is also an important consideration. For myself, what works best is two thirds grilling rack, one third griddle plate. I have the griddle plate on one side, which leaves plenty of space to spit roast or grill over the coals, while the remaining area is given over to griddle cooking.

To be honest, I've left the firemanship to the men in the family. I reckoned I had enough to do with marinating and skewering and all the other kitchen chores. But rest assured I have had my trial by fire. I don't think I would have ventured into print without getting soot on my hands, knowing the frustration of a fire that takes ages to get going and one that dies out half way through cooking.

There is something very satisfying about actually building a fire – it takes time, effort and requires you to use your wits in a way that setting a dial on an oven never does. And when the challenge has been met and the fire settles down to a bed of steady glowing coals, one is entitled to a sense of quiet pride. But getting a fire to the correct stage to cook on is a time-consuming business, taking from 45 minutes to 1 hour.

Some barbecues take only certain types of fuel and it is essential you follow the maker's instructions in this regard.

Charcoal lights more easily than compressed briquets, but also burns out faster.

Briquets or Heat Beads These are made of charcoal produced from hard woods which are ground, mixed with a binding material and pressed into a regular size and shape. They burn for a long time and give fairly even heat, but are not always easy to light. Even when lit, they take 45 minutes or more to reach the stage where they are ready for cooking over. Unlike charcoal, they don't glow red. Instead, when ready to cook on they are covered with a fine grey ash.

To build a fire with charcoal or briquets, start with a layer of coal about 5 cm (2 inches) deep with a fire-starter and a few twists of newspaper underneath. The coals should be laid lightly, with air spaces which will help the fire to take hold.

Light the paper and fire-starter and once the coals have started to burn, place more charcoal on the fire, taking into account what you intend to cook and the length of time it will take. Better to have too many coals than too few. It is such an anti-climax to be unable to finish the cooking and to start making the fire all over again.

Wood For a successful fire, the wood must be dry and hard, such as fruit wood or oak. Do not use soft, resinous wood such as pine or conifer. You will need plenty of wood for an effective source of cooking heat, as it burns quickly, and adding more wood in the middle of cooking is not advisable. Wait until the flames die down and cook only over the glowing embers. Build the fire with twigs and leaves as well as larger pieces of wood, and give it plenty of time to reach the desired stage. Wood can flare, and one good flare can burn the food.

Electric Barbecues These certainly don't have the charisma of wood and charcoal, but they are much more easily controlled. With an electric barbecue there are limitations such as how far you can go from the nearest power point.

Gas Barbecues The gas flame heats the volcanic or ceramic rock layer over the burners and food cooked over them does get a barbecued flavour due to the vaporising of the drips. Gas cylinders are portable so one isn't confined to having the barbecue in one place. Of course, a permanent barbecue set up can be piped into gas mains.

The most modern LP gas cylinders have a gauge which tells when it is due for refilling, otherwise have a second bottle on standby.

Have the store-check connections and fittings and learn the safety rules, as with any kind of barbecue.

FIRE AND HEAT CONTROL

One of the features that makes me appreciate my gas barbecue is that I can raise or lower the heat with a simple dial.

To control wood or coal fires, spread out the embers for less heat, or pile them together for more heat. Have a water spray handy and drench flare ups as they occur.

Check the fire at the end of cooking and make sure it is completely extinguished before you leave it.

NEVER pour inflammable liquid on a fire, even if it looks as though it will die in the middle of cooking. There is no help for it but to start over again, or try and add more charcoal at the edges of the fire so that it doesn't burn brightly under the food and char it.

To increase heat, open the damper and vent to create a draught if your unit operates with this system. To reduce heat reduce the openings, taking care not to shut them completely or you will extinguish the fire.

Another way is to raise or lower the grills so that the food is moved farther away from or closer to the fire.

My testing was done on a gas barbecue with a hood. Timings and amount of heat were as used under these conditions. If you are cooking without a hood (especially in cold weather or strong wind), the food will require longer cooking time. It is, in any case, better to watch the food and not the clock. To see if the food is cooked, check the colour, the firmness of the meat, the opacity of fish or seafood or the clearness of the juices that run when a skewer is inserted in a chicken thigh. (When cooked, the juices are clear, not pink.)

ACCESSORIES AND ADDITIONAL EQUIPMENT

Looking at the accessories and implements on sale at the barbecue shop, I realise one could spend a fortune and then find that some are not really useful.

Because I had some serious cooking to do in a limited period of time, I opted for a removable hood. This proved to be worth its weight in gold. When winds blow strong, they affect cooking times and heat control is virtually impossible without a hood or dome. Some people say that cooking under a hood is not true barbecuing, but I don't agree. Juices drop on the hot rocks and as they vaporise, impart that special outdoor flavour which doesn't happen when the heat is applied from above, as it is in a kitchen.

For extra flavour and aroma, we sometimes soak chips of mesquite or hickory and place them on the volcanic rock. The flavour of wood smoke and vaporising of juices combine to give food fabulous flavour. The fact that this happens under a protective hood does not detract from it at all.

Other suitable woods to use on the fire are prunings from grape vines and wood from fruit trees, but never use soft resinous woods, such as pine.

Buy good quality equipment, because flimsy tools will need replacing and are not economical in the long run. Among the indispensables are long-handled tongs and a spatula for turning food. Don't turn food with a fork because piercing the meat or poultry lets out the juices.

Buy basting brushes made of bristle, not nylon.

Metal skewers should be square or rectangular in cross section, not round. On round skewers the meat or other food is inclined to slip which makes it difficult to present different surfaces of the food to the heat. Long skewers with wooden handles are best.

Bamboo skewers are ideal for satays, kebabs or trussing poultry. **They must be soaked overnight or for at least 1 hour in cold water, to prevent them catching alight on the barbecue.**

A spit for rotisserie cooking is the ideal way to cook a large bird or leg of lamb, or large piece of beef. The rotisserie is fitted with a battery-operated motor which turns the food constantly, ensuring it cooks evenly from all sides. Very important for spit cooking are large prongs which hold the food steady.

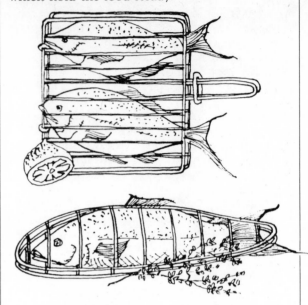

A hinged basket for cooking fish. Since fish is so fragile after it has been cooked, this is the best way of presenting it whole and perfectly done. The basket I use has a stand on both sides, so it is easy to turn it over. Without the handle it measures 40 cm (16 inches) and takes quite a large fish or two smaller fish such as trout.

A stiff wire brush with sharp scraper on the end, which is useful for cleaning the cooking surface.

Padded mitts for protecting hands.

Water spray, such as you would use for ironing or spraying indoor plants. Have it ready to drench flare-ups.

Meat thermometer. If cooking a large piece of meat or a turkey this would come in useful. Follow instructions as given with the thermometer.

Kebab turner. This is very useful, since a small motor keeps the kebabs in constant motion and therefore they cook evenly. This is only used with long metal skewers, not little bamboo ones.

STARTERS

What is it about outdoor cooking that makes everyone ravenous? It could be the fresh air, the appetising aromas, the involvement or just watching the barbecue cook getting on with the job.

What causes a ravenous appetite is not important, but how to deal with it is the essence of this chapter. Sure, you can prepare some little things on the barbecue, but don't rely on everything in the meal being cooked on the spot. If your fire doesn't get going as it should or if the barbecue is crowded just coping with the main meal, it makes sense to have some starters ready prepared. While those are being eaten and appreciated, barbecue other small appetisers which take very little time to fill the gaps while the main dish cooks.

As outdoor cooking is particularly suitable when the weather is brisk enough to make lingering near a fire a welcome prospect, the same brisk weather will contribute to ravenous appetites. What could be better than being ready with a pot of hearty soup? Use a heavy iron pot and put it on the barbecue to heat long before the coals are at that steady glowing stage needed for actually cooking.

In hot weather serve a cold soup – refreshing, yet enough to keep guests occupied and assuage any impatient appetites. Iced Gazpacho (see page 21) is particularly suitable when the temperature soars, and the ice cubes which are so welcome and important a feature can be kept ready in a wide-mouthed flask.

Some of the recipes which follow don't need cooking at all and others may be cooked beforehand. While there are some recipes particularly suitable for the barbecue, none of the recipes in this chapter requires lengthy cooking.

RUMAKI

Originating in Hawaii, this combination of flavour and texture has proved popular all over the world. Try for yourself the smoothness of chicken livers which contrasts against the crunchiness of water chestnuts.

Serves 6

3 tbsp shoyu (Japanese soy sauce)
1 tsp finely grated fresh ginger
1 garlic clove, crushed
2 tsp brown sugar
3 tbsp water
250 g (8 oz) chicken livers, trimmed and halved
1 × 250 g (8 oz) can water chestnuts, drained
125 g (4½ oz) streaky bacon rashers
wooden toothpicks

1. In a small saucepan, combine the shoyu, ginger, garlic, brown sugar and water. Bring to the boil, add the chicken livers and simmer on low heat for 2 minutes. Pour the marinade and livers into a flat dish and leave until cool. This brief cooking firms the livers, making them easier to handle, but they should still be pink and soft inside.

2. Halve the water chestnuts to make bite-sized pieces. Put a piece of chicken liver and water chestnut together, wrap with a strip of rindless bacon, and secure with a wooden toothpick. Alternatively, for ease of cooking, thread several on fine skewers so a number can be turned at once.

3. Grill at a good distance from the heat until the bacon is crisp and the liver heated through. Serve hot.

See photograph on page 26·27.

CRAB AND MUSHROOM SAVOURIES

A delectable mouthful (no cooking required) which may be made ahead to stave off the pangs of hunger during that seemingly interminable time between lighting the fire and it being ready for cooking.

Serves 6 (or more if there are other nibbles)

24 bite-sized mushroom caps
3 tbsp olive oil or salad oil
1 tbsp white wine vinegar
150 g (5 oz) frozen Alaskan crabmeat, defrosted
3 tbsp mayonnaise (see page 108)
3 tbsp finely chopped spring onion
salt and freshly ground black pepper, to taste
finely chopped parsley, to garnish

1. Gently remove the stems from the mushrooms and wipe the caps with a damp kitchen paper towel. Whisk the oil and vinegar together and use to brush the gills of the mushrooms. Place them on a platter with the stem side upwards.
2. In a bowl, flake the crabmeat, discarding any cartilage. Stir in the mayonnaise and spring onion, season to taste with salt and pepper and mix well. Pile the mixture onto the mushroom caps and sprinkle lightly with finely chopped parsley. Place on a serving dish or tray and chill until serving time.

SAVOURY PRUNES IN BACON

These savoury morsels don't take long to cook and may be placed around the outer edge of the grill until hot and crisp.

Serves 6

18 dessert prunes
3 tbsp fruit chutney
6 thin slices streaky bacon, rinded
wooden toothpicks

1. With a small pointed knife, slit each prune and remove the stone. Fill the cavity with a little fruit chutney.
2. Cut each bacon rasher into three lengths. Wrap each prune in a strip of bacon and secure with a wooden toothpick.
3. Grill on the cooler, outer edge of the barbecue, taking care the bacon fat doesn't drip directly onto the fire and cause flare-ups. Serve warm.

See photograph on page 26·27.

BARBECUED HONEY PRAWNS

The flavours of this popular Chinese dish remain the same, but instead of being dipped in batter and deep fried, the prawns are threaded onto skewers and grilled.

Serves 4

500 g (1 lb) large raw prawns
1 garlic clove, crushed
¼ tsp salt
4 tbsp soy sauce
2 tbsp sherry
1 tbsp honey
4 tbsp sesame seeds, toasted
bamboo skewers, soaked for 1 hour

1. Shell and devein the prawns, rinse, then pat dry on kitchen paper.
2. Combine the garlic, salt, soy sauce, sherry and honey in a bowl. Add the prawns and marinate for 20 minutes or longer. Thread them onto bamboo skewers, leaving half of each skewer free. Sprinkle over the sesame seeds and press on firmly.
3. Barbecue the prawns over gently glowing coals on an oiled grid, taking care not to overcook. Brush with the marinade frequently and turn the skewers after 2 or 3 minutes. The prawns are done when they look opaque.

COOK'S TIP
Toast the sesame seeds in a dry pan over medium heat stirring constantly. Turn out of the pan and cool.

TAHITIAN-STYLE MARINATED FISH

Don't tell the more timid among your guests that the fish is raw – they'll never guess. This delicately flavoured entrée is usually the most popular item at a party, but make sure the fish is fresh, not frozen.

Serves 4–6

| 500 g (1 lb) fillets of firm white fish |
| juice of 3 or 4 lemons |
| ½ tsp salt |
| 4 shallots or salad onions, thinly sliced |
| 2 firm ripe tomatoes, diced |
| 1 small green cucumber, diced |
| 100 g (4 oz) creamed coconut |
| 125 ml (4½ fl oz) hot water |
| freshly ground white pepper, to taste |
| lettuce cups, to serve |

1. Remove all the skin from the fish fillets and rinse under cold running water, making sure there are no scales or bones left. Pat dry on kitchen paper. Wash the knife and board you are using and cut the fish into dice or short strips.
2. Strain the lemon juice into a shallow bowl. Put in the fish, sprinkle with the salt, add the onions and mix well. The lemon juice should cover the fish. Cover with cling film and marinate the fish overnight in the refrigerator, or for at least 6 hours, turning it over once or twice with a non-metal spoon.
3. Before serving, drain away the lemon juice and combine the fish with the tomatoes and cucumber. To make the dressing, dissolve the coconut cream in the water and cool. Season to taste with salt and pepper and pour it over the fish. Spoon the mixture into the lettuce cups and serve.

SERVING SUGGESTION ---

For a particularly colourful presentation, garnish the salad with slices of peeled kiwi fruit and tiny red radish roses.

SPICY STEAMED MUSSELS

Mussels don't take long to cook, so it is a good idea to make the spiced base beforehand and finish cooking it over the barbecue. Do not use any mussels that are not tightly closed when raw. Scrub mussels well and beard them (pull the little tuft firmly away from the hinge of the shell.) Keep them cool in a bucket until ready to cook, and discard any that don't open during cooking.

Serves 4

| 3 tbsp ghee (clarified butter), or oil |
| 2 onions, finely chopped |
| 2 garlic cloves, crushed |
| 1 tbsp finely chopped fresh ginger |
| 2 red chillies, seeded and chopped, optional |
| 1 tsp ground turmeric |
| 1 tbsp ground coriander |
| ½ tsp salt |
| 250 ml (8 fl oz) water |
| 1 kg (2 lb) fresh mussels, cleaned |
| 2 tbsp chopped fresh coriander leaves |
| juice of half a lemon |

1. Heat the ghee in a large, deep saucepan and fry the onions, garlic and ginger over medium heat, stirring occasionally, until soft and golden. Add the chillies if using, turmeric and ground coriander, and cook, stirring, for 3 minutes.
2. Add the salt and water to the pan, bring to the boil, cover and simmer for 5 minutes. The recipe may be prepared ahead up to this point.
3. When ready to cook the mussels bring the spiced liquid back to the boil, add the mussels, cover the pan tightly and cook on the grill or plate for 10–12 minutes or until the shells have opened.
4. Remove from the heat, sprinkle in the coriander leaves and lemon juice. Taste and adjust the seasoning if necessary. Serve the mussels in deep bowls or soup plates with crusty bread for soaking up the sauce.

See photograph on page 25

CHINESE MUSHROOM, CHICKEN AND PORK SAUSAGE

Dried Chinese mushrooms have a distinctive flavour and cannot be replaced with European-style mushrooms. They are expensive, but only a small amount need be purchased and they keep indefinitely.

Serves 8–10 as an hors d'oeuvre

25 g (1 oz) dried Chinese mushrooms (doong gwoo)

500 g (1 lb) chicken breast fillets

250 g (8 oz) Chinese barbecued pork or roast pork

1 × 230 g (8 oz) can water chestnuts

1 garlic clove, crushed

1 tsp salt

½ tsp freshly ground black pepper

½ tsp five-spice powder

1 tsp finely grated fresh ginger

2 tbsp Chinese wine or dry sherry

1 tbsp sesame oil

2 tbsp soy sauce

1 tbsp cornflour

1 tbsp hoi sin sauce or Oriental barbecue sauce

sausage skin, large size and about 1 m (3 ft) in length

1. Soak the mushrooms in very hot water for at least 30 minutes, by which time they should have doubled in size and be quite soft. Cut off and discard the tough stems and chop the mushroom caps finely.
2. Remove any skin from the chicken and dice the meat. Dice the barbecued pork.
3. Drain the water chestnuts and chop finely. Put all the diced and chopped ingredients into a large bowl. In another small bowl, combine all the seasonings, wine, oil, soy sauce, garlic, ginger and cornflour. Mix thoroughly, pour over the contents of the large bowl and mix with your hands well.
4. Tie a knot in one end of the sausage skin and cut off a length of about 1 m (3 ft). Using a funnel, push the filling into the sausage skin. Either coil the sausage around or twist the skin at intervals to form small sausages. Place the sausage in an oiled barbecue basket and prick the skin with a very fine sharp skewer (poultry pins are ideal) to prevent bursting.
5. Cook the sausage over glowing coals at a good distance from the heat, until golden brown on one side, then turn and grill the other side.

COOK'S TIP

Barbecued pork can be bought ready cooked in Chinatown, if not, use a fatty portion of cold roast pork.

MUSHROOMS WITH GARLIC BUTTER

No vegetable is simpler to cook on a barbecue. Just remember not to turn the mushrooms over or you'll lose all the melted butter.

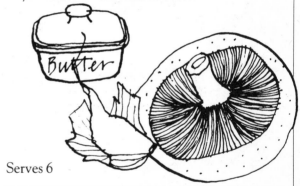

Serves 6

18 large firm mushrooms

60 g (2½ oz) butter, softened

1 garlic clove, crushed with ½ tsp sea salt

wooden toothpicks

1. Trim the ends of mushroom stems and wipe over the caps with damp kitchen paper. Don't wash the mushrooms or they'll lose flavour and absorb water.
2. Mix the butter with the garlic and form into a small pat on a square of aluminium foil. Place in the freezer and chill until firm. Cut into 18 pieces.
3. Attach a piece of butter to the stem of the upturned mushroom with a wooden toothpick. Place on a lightly oiled griddle plate or over the grill until the butter melts and the mushrooms soften. Slip a frying spoon under each mushroom and transfer to plates.

See photograph on page 26·27.

HEARTY FIRESIDE SOUP

A thick vegetable soup made the day before and reheated over the fire is a great way to start a barbecue and stave off starvation while the main course cooks. If the weather changes, bring the soup in. Either way it will be a great start to the meal.

Serves 6

250 g (8 oz) dried haricot beans

3 tbsp olive oil

3 large garlic cloves, crushed

2 large leeks, washed well and thinly sliced

1 medium-sized onion, sliced

1 large carrot, scrubbed and diced

1 stalk celery, diced

½ tsp finely chopped fresh rosemary

1 tsp dried basil

1 tbsp tomato paste

125 ml (4½ fl oz) hot water or vegetable stock

1 whole clove

salt and freshly ground black pepper, to taste

¼ cabbage, finely shredded

4 small, firm courgettes (zucchini), trimmed and cut into thick slices

100 g (4 oz) pasta or rice, cooked

1. Soak the beans overnight, or put them into a large saucepan with plenty of water to cover and bring to the boil. Turn off the heat and leave, covered for 2 hours.
2. Change the water and bring to the boil once more. Simmer for an hour or until the beans are tender. Drain the beans, reserving the water.
3. Heat the olive oil in a large heavy-based pan and add the garlic, leek, onion, carrot, celery and herbs. Stir well until the vegetables are lightly coated with oil, then turn the heat very low, cover the pan and sweat the vegetables for 15–20 minutes. They should not be allowed to brown.
4. In a blender or food processor, purée about a third of the beans with their cooking liquid and add it to the vegetables. Stir in the tomato paste blended with the water or stock, together with the remaining whole beans, whole clove and salt and pepper to taste.
5. When the soup returns to the boil, add the cabbage and courgettes and cook for 20 minutes longer or until all the vegetables are tender. The soup should be thick and stick-to-the-ribs, but if required, add a little more hot water or stock. Add the pasta then serve hot in thick mugs with crisp breadsticks or fingers of fried bread.

ICED GAZPACHO

How can a cold soup be a hot favourite? I only know that it is, especially on a warm summer day.

Serves 6

1 kg (2 lb) ripe tomatoes, peeled and seeded

2 green cucumbers

2 capsicum (sweet peppers)

1 small onion, chopped

1 garlic clove, crushed

60 g (2½ oz) fresh breadcrumbs

750 ml (1¼ pt) cold water

4 tbsp red wine vinegar

4 tbsp olive oil

salt and freshly ground black pepper, to taste

olive oil for frying

4 thin slices white bread, crusts removed and diced

1. Dice four tomatoes. Halve one cucumber lengthways, seed and dice. Dice one capsicum. Reserve each diced vegetable for the garnish in separate bowls, cover and chill until required.
2. Put the onion into a blender or food processor with the remaining tomatoes, cucumber, capsicum, garlic and breadcrumbs. Blend to a purée, adding some of the water if required.
3. Pour the mixture into a large bowl and stir in the water, vinegar, olive oil, salt and pepper. Cover tightly with a lid or cling film and chill for at least 2 hours.
4. Heat a little oil in a frying pan and fry the bread until golden, then drain on absorbent kitchen paper. Cool and store in an airtight container.
5. To serve, ladle the soup into bowls with a couple of ice cubes added, or present it in one large bowl. Either way, pass the small bowls of garnishes and crisp croûtons separately.

CROSTINI ALLA MOZZARELLA

Delectable proof that bread and cheese is not just for children's school lunches. When shopping, look for bread which is slightly larger in diameter than the cheese.

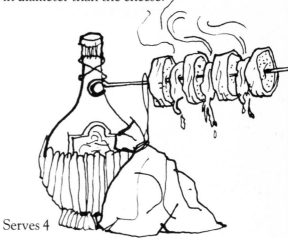

Serves 4

60 g (2½ oz) butter, melted

2 tbsp olive oil

2 tbsp finely chopped chives

2 tbsp finely chopped flat leaf parsley

16 round slices of crusty Italian or French bread, thickly sliced

12 medium thick slices Mozzarella cheese

4 canned fillets of anchovy, boned and mashed

extra flat leaf parsley, to garnish

1. Mix the melted butter and olive oil and use half to mix with the chopped herbs. Lightly brush onto both sides of the bread slices, taking care not to let too much oil soak in. Thread alternate slices of bread and cheese, onto four skewers, beginning and ending with a slice of bread. Push the slices together firmly.
2. Turn the skewers over gently glowing coals (a wood fire with aromatic twigs or chips of hickory gives great flavour) until the bread is lightly toasted and the cheese starts to melt. I find a rotisserie attachment is ideal as it keeps the bread and cheese turning constantly, so the cheese doesn't fall off in blobs.
3. Mix the anchovies with the remaining butter and oil, and spoon over the crostini when they have been transferred to individual plates. Serve hot, garnished with a few sprigs of flat leaf parsley and accompanied by tomato slices.

See photograph on page 28.

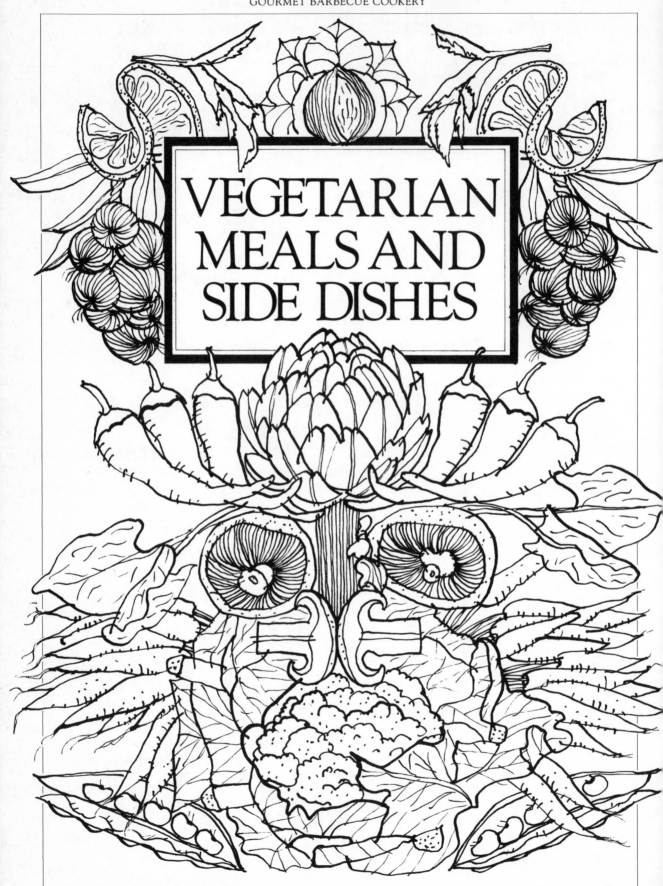

VEGETARIAN MEALS AND SIDE DISHES

Amouthful of a chapter heading, but there are two distinct types of recipes. Some are main dishes that amply fill the needs of a barbecue meal without meat. Others are delicious ways of cooking vegetables to serve as accompaniments.

One of the advantages of a vegetarian barbecue is that you can stage it at a moment's notice. It won't matter if it is the weekend and the shops are shut – if you have potatoes and cheese in the cupboard, and herbs growing in the garden, you can offer guests a fantastic speciality, Potato Shells with Cheese and Herbs (see page 29). You wouldn't think that potatoes and cheese cooked on a barbecue and brushed with herbed oil or butter could be so special, but it is. Served with thick slices of ripe tomato or a salad of roasted capsicums (peppers), with chilled wine to sip, it is a meal you and your guests will enjoy, *and* it's nutritionally sound.

For the health conscious, there are perfectly balanced high protein-low fat recipes based on dried beans and lentils. High in flavour too, so surprise your friends who do eat meat with an alternative they may not have thought of before.

'BAKED' MUSHROOMS

Serve these cooked mushrooms in individual aluminium foil packets to be opened on each guest's plate. Flavoured butter can be used.

Serves 4

| 4 tsp butter |
| 1 medium-sized onion, thinly sliced |
| 16 medium-sized mushrooms, wiped and trimmed |
| salt and freshly ground black pepper, to taste |

1. On 4 squares of heavy duty aluminium foil, place a pat of butter, some onion slices, and then the mushrooms. Season with a good grinding of salt and pepper. Gather up the foil and fold the edges together to seal. Barbecue for 10–15 minutes, depending on the distance from the heat. Serve as an accompaniment to grilled meats, fish or other vegetables.

FRESH BUTTERED CORN ON THE COB

Sweet, fresh corn on the cob is something totally enjoyable – but it must be tender and young to start with because no amount of cooking can redeem those that have been sitting around for too long.

Serves 4

| 4 ears of fresh corn |
| 4 tsp cold butter |
| freshly ground salt and black pepper, to taste |

1. Gently pull back the corn husks and remove the cornsilk. Soak in cold water for ½–1 hour, shake off excess water and spread 1 tsp of cold butter over the kernels of each. Season to taste with salt and pepper and replace the husks over the corn. Twist a bit of wire around the tip to hold the husks in place.
2. Place the corn cobs around the edges of the barbecue where the heat is low and cook for 20 minutes or until tender. The outer husks will have burned, but the inner ones will keep the corn moist. A little colour on the kernels imparts that delicious barbecued flavour. Remove from the heat with tongs and use gloves to twist off the wire and remove the husks. Serve hot, with extra butter for those who want it.

— COOK'S TIP —
Cook the corn without the butter if preferred, or with a flavoured butter such as garlic or herb. If liked, the cobs may be wrapped in aluminium foil, but I think the best flavour is achieved without it.

CRUSTY CARAMELISED ONION RINGS

Onions cooking and browning provide another dimension to any meal . . . the aroma alone is most tempting.

Serves 4

3 tbsp oil
2 large mild onions, thickly sliced
2 tbsp Barbecue Sauce Americana

1. Heat the barbecue griddle or a heavy iron frying pan, and add the oil.
2. Cook the onions slowly until translucent, turning them over until golden brown. Pour the sauce over, tossing the onions quickly then transfer to a plate as the heat will caramelise the sauce. Serve as an accompaniment to meat, poultry or lentil burgers.

TOMATOES WITH CRISPY GARLIC CRUMBS

When these are cooked in the oven the crumbs make a crisp topping, but on a barbecue you need to cheat a little and fry the crumbs first.

Serves 4

4 firm, ripe tomatoes
salt and freshly ground black pepper, to taste
60 g (2½ oz) butter
2 garlic cloves, crushed
125 g (4½ oz) fresh breadcrumbs

1. Cut the tomatoes in half crossways and squeeze gently to remove the seeds. Season with salt and pepper.
2. In a small pan, heat the butter and sauté the garlic and breadcrumbs until golden and crisp.
3. Cook the tomatoes on the edge of the barbecue where the heat is not too fierce, and when they are almost done, spoon the crisp crumbs onto each one and serve.

MIXED VEGETABLE MEDLEY

A selection of vegetables without the hassle of cooking each one separately. Use a double layer of aluminium foil to prevent scorching.

Serves 4

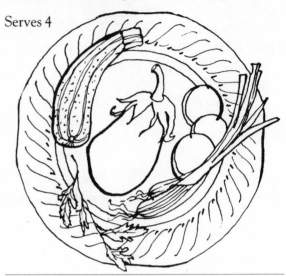

1 yam or sweet potato, thickly sliced
1 small aubergine (eggplant), thickly sliced
2 courgettes (zucchini) cut into sixths lengthways
2 spring onions, cut into short lengths
1 tbsp raspberry vinegar
1 tsp caster sugar

1. Blanch the yam in boiling water for 5 minutes and the aubergine for 2 minutes. Divide all the vegetables between four pieces of aluminium foil.
2. Stir the vinegar and sugar together until the sugar has dissolved, then sprinkle a little of the mixture over the vegetables. Fold the edges on top of the parcel together to seal and barbecue for 15 minutes on medium hot coals.

Spicy steamed mussels (page 18) and Pumpkins with bechamel prawns (page 40).

OVERLEAF
Left to right: Potato shells with cheese and herbs (page 29); Mushrooms with garlic butter (page 19); Red, green and yellow capsicums (page 126); Rumaki (page 16) and Savoury prunes in bacon (page 17); Aubergine fans with tomato, onion and olives (page 31).

POTATOES AU NATURELLE

No recipe needed, really, just a reminder that for the best results your potatoes must be well scrubbed and dried, then rubbed with a little butter or oil before being wrapped in aluminium foil. Press the foil closely around the potato to exclude air. Place on the barbecue grill or on coals and allow sufficient time for them to cook through. Medium-sized potatoes are best. Unwrap, break open and season with salt and pepper or top with a pat of butter, spoonful of soured cream, or sprinkling of herbs.

POTATO SHELLS WITH CHEESE AND HERBS

Potatoes with a savoury filling like this make a good main dish for vegetarians. They are also irresistible to others who already have a chop or chicken joint on the plate.

Serves 8

| 8 large potatoes, scrubbed |
| 4 tbsp melted butter |
| 2 medium-sized leeks, washed well and finely shredded or 2 onions, chopped |
| 2 garlic cloves, crushed |
| 2 tbsp chopped fresh coriander or mint |
| 2 tbsp chopped fresh dill |
| 250 g (8 oz) ricotta or cottage cheese |
| 2 hard boiled eggs, peeled and diced |
| ½ tsp ground allspice |
| ¼ tsp ground cloves |
| ¼ tsp freshly grated nutmeg |
| 2 tsp made mustard |
| 2 tsp Worcestershire sauce |
| 25 g (1 oz) fresh wholemeal breadcrumbs |
| salt and freshly ground black pepper, to taste |
| sprig of dill or snipped chives, to garnish |

Crostini alla mozzarella (page 21) with Mange tout, water chestnuts and raddichio salad (page 94).

Soured Cream Dressing

| 250 ml (8 fl oz) thick soured cream |
| 250 ml (8 fl oz) natural yoghurt |
| 1 garlic clove, crushed with ½ tsp salt |
| 1 tbsp chopped fresh dill |
| 2 tbsp chopped chives, optional |

1. Try to buy flattish potatoes – they are much easier to fill and will sit more securely on the barbecue. Boil the potatoes in their skins for 10 minutes, drain and leave until cool enough to handle.
2. Cut the potatoes in half lengthways and scoop out the centres, leaving shells about 1 cm (½ in) thick. Boil the centres until soft, then drain, mash and reserve for the filling.
3. Brush the potato shells inside and out with melted butter and place on squares of double thickness aluminium foil.
4. Heat the remaining butter in a pan and fry the leeks until soft. Add the garlic and fresh herbs and stir over low heat for a couple of minutes longer. Remove from the heat.
5. Mix the reserved mashed potato, cheese and egg into the onion mixture. Add the spices, mustard, Worcestershire sauce, breadcrumbs, salt and freshly ground pepper to taste. Fill the potato shells, mounding the mixture slightly.
6. Bring the foil together at the top and fold the edges over to form a parcel. Barbecue for 30–40 minutes, until done, depending on the size of the potatoes.

Meanwhile, make the sour cream dressing: combine the soured cream and yoghurt in a bowl, stir in the garlic and herbs and season to taste.

To serve, unfold the parcels and spoon the soured cream dressing over the potatoes. Garnish with a small sprig of fresh dill or a few snipped chives.

See photograph on page 26·27.

ROQUEFORT POTATOES

This may seem an extravagant way to use a really good blue cheese, but I can promise you it does something for the humble spud.

Serves 4

4 medium large potatoes, scrubbed
60 g (2½ oz) Roquefort or other creamy blue cheese
1 tbsp soured cream
freshly ground salt and black pepper

1. Cook the potatoes in boiling water until tender, drain, then cut in halves. Do not peel. When cool enough to handle, scoop out the centres, leaving a thick shell.
2. In a bowl, mash the potato scooped out from the shells. With a fork, mash the Roquefort until smooth (if using a cheese with a crust, mash it in with the cheese) and mix it into the potatoes. Add the soured cream, salt and pepper to taste and mix well. Fill the potato shells.
3. Depending on the type of barbecue, it may be necessary to protect the potato by wrapping at least the bottom half in aluminium foil. Place on the barbecue and cook until heated through.

SWEET POTATOES WITH GRAND MARNIER

Orange flavoured and slightly spicy, these root vegetables belie their humble beginnings and go well with steaks, chops or poultry.

Serves 4

500 g (1 lb) sweet potatoes
4 tbsp brown sugar
4 tbsp orange juice
1 tbsp honey
1 tbsp Grand Marnier
½ tsp finely grated orange rind
pinch of freshly grated nutmeg

1. Boil the sweet potatoes for 10 minutes or until half tender, drain immediately, cool and peel. Cut into thick slices and divide among 4 double squares of heavy duty aluminium foil.
2. Combine the rest of the ingredients in a bowl and spoon a little over each quantity of sweet potato. Fold the edges of the parcels to seal and place on the edge of the barbecue where the heat is not fierce enough to cause the sugar to burn on the bottom of the parcel. Cook until the potatoes are tender.

CORN AND AUBERGINE KEBABS

Since corn takes longer to cook than aubergine, it needs a little pre-cooking before joining its companion on the barbecue.

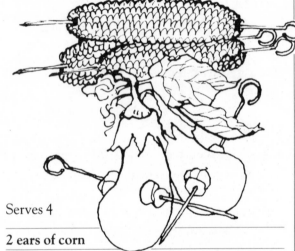

Serves 4

2 ears of corn
1 aubergine (eggplant), the same diameter as the corn
60 ml (2½ fl oz) garlic dressing (see page 107)
salt and freshly ground pepper, to taste
bamboo skewers, soaked for 1 hour

1. Pre-cook the corn until almost tender, either in boiling water with a pinch of sugar added for 6–8 minutes, or in the microwave oven.
2. Drain the corn and cut it into chunky slices. Cut the aubergine into slices about 1 cm (½ inch) thick and marinate them in the garlic dressing for 10 minutes.
3. Thread alternate slices of corn and aubergine onto skewers and season with salt and pepper. Barbecue on the grill until the aubergine is tender and the corn lightly coloured, about 5 minutes, turning the skewers so they cook on all sides.

AUBERGINE FANS WITH TOMATO, ONION AND OLIVES

A pretty dish, and worth a little preparation.

Serves 4

2 medium-sized aubergines (eggplants)
3 tbsp olive oil
1 medium-sized onion, finely sliced
2 ripe tomatoes, sliced
1 tbsp chopped parsley
salt and freshly ground black pepper, to taste
60 ml (2½ fl oz) water
60 g (2½ oz) black olives
2 tbsp capers, chopped
1 × 400 g (14 oz) can artichoke hearts, halved

1. Wash the aubergines but do not peel them. With a stainless steel knife, cut off the stalk and cut it in half lengthways. Place the cut surface downwards on a board and slice thinly lengthways from the bottom to within 2 cm (¾ inch) of the top to make a fan.
2. Place the aubergine in a baking dish brushed with the olive oil and insert slices of onion and tomato between the slices of aubergine.
3. Sprinkle with the parsley and trickle the remaining olive oil over. Grind the salt and pepper over the vegetables, pour the water into a corner of the dish, and scatter the olives, capers and artichoke hearts on top. Cover with aluminium foil and bake on the barbecue for about an hour or until the vegetables are tender.

See photograph on page 26·27.

PUMPKIN VEGETABLE MEDLEY

This has received an enthusiastic seal of approval from my resident teenage critic, *and* it's a great way to use up leftover vegetables.

Serves 2

2 golden nugget pumpkins, or about 500 g (1 lb) butternut pumpkin or squash
1 cooked potato, diced
60 g (2½ oz) green beans, broccoli or asparagus, blanched and diced
90 g (3½ oz) Cheddar cheese, diced

Quick Béchamel

1 tbsp butter
1 small shallot, finely chopped
1½ tbsp flour
250 ml (8 fl oz) milk
1 bay leaf
¼ tsp celery salt
pinch white pepper

1. Cut off the top third of each nugget pumpkin or, if using a butternut pumpkin, halve lengthways. With a spoon, scoop out and discard all the seeds and fibres. Bake in a hot oven for 30 minutes or until almost tender.
2. Melt the butter in a heavy based saucepan, add the shallot and cook until soft, then add the flour and cook, stirring, for 1 minute. Add the milk and bay leaf and whisk over low heat until the sauce boils and becomes smooth and thick. Season with the celery salt and the white pepper. Remove and discard the bay leaf. Add the diced cheese.
3. Fill the cavity of the pumpkin with the potato and green vegetable, then pour in the sauce. Replace the pumpkin lid and wrap in aluminium foil.
4. Barbecue the pumpkins over slow heat for 25–30 minutes or until the filling has heated through and the cheese melted. Serve in the foil.

SUNNY PUMPKIN BAKE

I've been cooking for a vegetarian teenager for four years, and this kind of recipe is one of the reasons he doesn't feel left out at a barbecue. Also, I know he's getting enough protein.

Serves 4

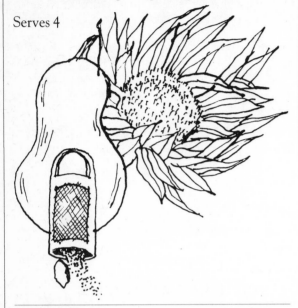

| 1 butternut pumpkin, about 750 g (1½ lb) |
| freshly ground sea salt and black pepper |
| ¼ tsp freshly grated nutmeg |
| 25 g (1 oz) butter |
| 1 large onion, finely chopped |
| 1 tbsp olive oil |
| 125 g (4½ oz) cottage cheese |
| 2 tbsp sunflower kernels |

1. Cut the pumpkin in two lengthways. Scoop out and discard the seeds and membrane. Cook the pumpkin shells until half tender, either by steaming over water, baking in a hot oven, or in a microwave oven.

2. When cool enough to handle, scoop out some of the flesh from the centre of the pumpkin, using a curved grapefruit knife or a spoon. Return the scooped out pumpkin to the pan or microwave and continue to cook until soft, then drain off the excess liquid and mash until smooth, adding salt and pepper to taste, nutmeg and butter.

3. Cook the onion in the olive oil over low heat until soft but not brown. Mix it into the mashed pumpkin together with the cottage cheese and sunflower kernels. Fill the pumpkin shells with the mixture. Prepare ahead up to this point.

4. When barbecuing, place the pumpkin on the grill over medium coals and cook for about 15 minutes or until the pumpkin is tender and the filling has heated through.

COOK'S TIP

You may like to mould a sheet of aluminium foil around the pumpkin shell for easier handling. It is not necessary to cover the top.

PUMPKIN AND ONION PAPILLOTES

This is a versatile recipe which can serve any number of people. For this reason I have deliberately avoided giving quantities so they can be adjusted to suit the size of any party.

| butternut pumpkin, unpeeled |
| onion, thickly sliced |
| salt and freshly ground black pepper, to taste |

1. Cut the pumpkin into thick slices and remove any seeds and membrane in the centre. Place some onion rings on top and season to taste with salt and pepper. Wrap in aluminium foil and barbecue over medium hot coals until tender, about 35 minutes.

HONEY-ROAST PUMPKIN SLICES

Thick slices of pumpkin roasted on the barbecue go well with barbecued meat or poultry, or with some of the lentil-based dishes.

Serves 4

| 4 thick slices of pumpkin, with skin left on |
| 2 tbsp honey |
| 3 tbsp oil |
| sea salt, to taste |

1. If you can get a butternut pumpkin, cut round slices from the narrow portion where the vegetable is solid and there are no seeds. If using

other types of pumpkin or squash, scoop out and discard the seeds and membrane.

2. Place the pumpkin on the grill and barbecue until almost tender, then brush with the honey and oil which has been mixed together. This will make a nice caramel coating on the pumpkin. Serve with a sprinkling of sea salt.

SOUTH SEA ISLAND SPINACH

One of the joys of holidays spent cruising among the islands of the South Pacific is investigating the local cuisine, going to the markets and tasting everything from fresh fruits to breadfruit roasted in the coals. On one of these visits we discovered *palusami*, or young taro leaves with coconut cream, wrapped in breadfruit leaves and cooked over the coals. This recipe can be recreated using spinach . . . the flavour is almost identical. The only difference is that we use aluminium foil for wrapping.

Serves 4

1 large bunch spinach or chard (silver beet)
1 large onion, thinly sliced
125 ml (4½ fl oz) thick coconut milk (see page 125)
salt, to taste

1. Wash the spinach well in cold water, making sure all sand has been rinsed out. Cut off the stems. If using chard, strip the leaves away from the white stalks.

2. Bring a large pan of water to the boil and blanch the leaves a few at a time, holding them in the water for about half a minute. They don't have to be cooked, merely softened sufficiently to make compact parcels. Drain in a colander.

3. Take two lengths of heavy duty aluminium foil. In the middle of each, place another piece of foil folded double to protect the bottom of the parcel from scorching. Put some spinach leaves on the double foil, bunching them in a neat pile in the centre. Add a few slices of onion on top, then season with a little salt. Repeat until all the spinach and onion have been used. Do not use too much salt – the flavour should be mild and sweet.

4. Spoon the coconut milk over the spinach. Bring the foil together at the top and fold over twice to seal the edges. Cook on the barbecue for 6–8 minutes. Each parcel should give 2 servings.

COURGETTES PROVENÇALE

Vegetables which cook in a short time are particularly suitable for preparing on a barbecue, either in aluminium foil trays or in a heavy iron frying pan with a handle moulded all in one.

Serves 6

3 tbsp olive oil
1 garlic clove, crushed
2 ripe tomatoes, seeded and diced
salt and freshly ground black pepper, to taste
6 medium sized courgettes (zucchini), trimmed and thickly sliced
chopped parsley, to garnish

1. Heat the oil in a frying pan and gently sauté the garlic. Add the tomatoes and stir well, then add the courgette and season with salt and pepper. Cover with a lid or aluminium foil and cook on the cooler outside edge of the barbecue plate until the courgette is tender when pierced with a fork. Just before serving, sprinkle with chopped parsley.

COOK'S TIP

If the mixture starts to sizzle while cooking add a little water.

LENTIL, SESAME AND SUNFLOWER BURGERS

So good to eat and good for you too! We cook these often, pan-frying them rather than reserving them for barbecues only. As a main meal, serve them with lightly steamed vegetables or a salad.

Serves 6

125 g (4 oz) brown lentils

125 g (4 oz) red lentils

500 ml (17 fl oz) water

1 tbsp yeast extract

2 tbsp soy sauce

1 egg, beaten

1 tsp dried oregano or marjoram

1 tsp curry powder, optional

1 tbsp honey

1 garlic clove, crushed

1 large carrot, grated

1 large onion, grated

1 large potato, grated

50 g (2 oz) sunflower seeds

40 g (1½ oz) sesame seeds

125 g (4 oz) oats

4 tbsp wholemeal flour

hamburger rolls, shredded lettuce, mayonnaise, to serve

1. Pick over the lentils then wash well and drain. Put into a saucepan with the water and bring to the boil, then turn off the heat and leave to soak for 2 hours. Add the yeast extract and cook, covered, until all water has been absorbed and the lentils are soft.

2. Mix the soy sauce, egg, herbs and seasonings together. In a large bowl, combine all the remaining ingredients thoroughly, adding in the egg mixture.

3. Form the mixture into hamburger shapes. Heat the griddle plate of the barbecue, brush with a little oil and cook the burgers over low coals until golden brown on both sides. Serve on hamburger rolls with the shredded lettuce and mayonnaise (see page 108).

CHICK PEA AND NUT BURGERS

When vegetarian food tastes like this, nobody feels deprived if you surprise them with a non-meat barbecue.

Serves 6

200 g (7 oz) dried chick peas (garbanzo beans), soaked overnight

2 tbsp oil

2 onions, finely chopped

1 garlic clove, crushed

2 tsp curry powder

salt and freshly ground black pepper

60 g (2½ oz) chopped almonds

60 g (2½ oz) chopped walnuts

60 g (2½ oz) toasted sunflower seeds

100 g (4 oz) flour

2 eggs, beaten

100 g (4 oz) dry breadcrumbs

oil, for brushing

mayonnaise, to serve

1. Wash the dried chick peas, put them into a saucepan with plenty of unsalted water to cover and bring to the boil. Simmer in the covered pan for 2 hours or until very soft, then drain thoroughly in a colander.

2. Heat the oil and gently soften the onion and garlic, stirring occasionally until golden – this step may not seem important but makes a great deal of difference to the flavour.

3. Mash the chick peas until smooth, using a

food processor or blender if available. Mix in with the sautéed onions and garlic, curry powder, salt and pepper to taste, and the chopped nuts and sunflower seeds. Form into round patties and coat in the flour, then in beaten egg and finally in dry breadcrumbs.

4. Heat and lightly oil the griddle plate on your barbecue, or use a large iron frying pan and coat the base with a little oil. Cook the burgers over medium hot coals until golden on one side, then flip over with a frying slice and cook the other side. Serve warm or cold, topped with a spoonful of creamy mayonnaise (see page 108).

COOK'S TIP

If there's room on the griddle plate cook thick slices of tomato to go with them.

TACOS WITH CHILLI BEANS AND CHEESE

These Mexican favourites are ideal for meatless main dishes at a barbecue. The tacos crisp and heat through in an aluminium foil container and are then topped with shredded lettuce and diced tomato. For those who like it hot, pass taco sauce.

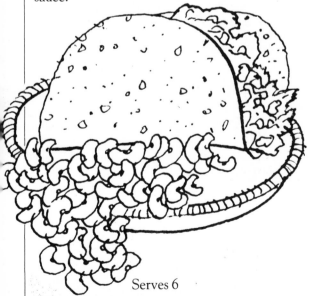

Serves 6

12 taco shells

shredded lettuce, diced tomatoes and taco sauce or garlic dressing (see page 107), to serve

Spicy Kidney Bean Filling

500 g (1 lb) dried kidney beans, soaked overnight

2 medium-sized onions, finely sliced

2 garlic cloves, crushed

1 dried chilli, seeded

2 ripe tomatoes, seeded and chopped

1 tsp salt

½ tsp freshly ground black pepper

1 tsp ground cumin

3 tbsp oil

1. The day before cooking, prepare the bean filling. Put the soaked kidney beans in a large pan with water to cover, one onion, garlic and chilli. Bring to the boil, reduce the heat and simmer for 1 hour. Add the salt, pepper, cumin and 1 tbsp of the oil and continue cooking until the beans are very soft and almost all the liquid has been absorbed. Stir occasionally to prevent the beans sticking to the pan.

2. In another large pan, heat the remaining oil and fry the other onion until soft but not brown. Add the tomatoes and simmer for a few minutes, then add the drained beans. Mash with a wooden spoon or potato masher and cook until they are a thick paste. Remove from the heat, adjust the seasoning if necessary and reserve until required.

3. Reheat the reserved bean filling. Place the taco shells on the barbecue to heat through, then move them aside. Spoon some of the bean mixture into each shell, then put a little shredded lettuce, some coarsely grated cheese and diced tomato on top. If liked, add a spoonful of taco sauce, or perhaps a dollop of garlic dressing.

COOK'S TIP

Tacos are eaten out of the hand, and paper plates are in order. Have lettuce, cheese, tomatoes and sauce ready arranged on a divided platter or in separate bowls placed on a tray and let everybody help themselves.

WHEAT AND RICE PILAF

Using whole wheat kernels (or wheat berries as they are called in the U.S.) in combination with long grain rice, gives the pilaf a totally different look and texture. You *must* soak the wheat overnight as described or it will be too hard to eat.

Serves 6

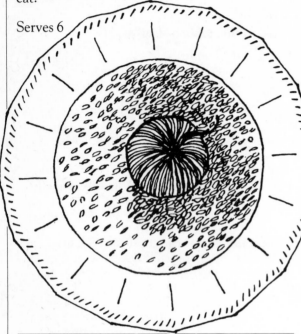

125 g (4 oz) whole wheat kernels
500 g (1 lb) long grain white rice
3 tbsp ghee (clarified butter)
1 large onion, finely sliced
1 quill cinnamon, optional
1 lt (1¾ pts) hot chicken stock
2 tsp salt
½ tsp freshly ground black pepper
1 tbsp butter
125 g (4 oz) slivered almonds or raw cashews

1. The night before the pilaf is required, wash the wheat, put it into a saucepan with water to cover and bring it to the boil. Have ready a wide-mouthed vacuum flask and pour in the wheat and as much water as the flask will hold, cover tightly and leave overnight. Alternatively, cook the wheat for 30 minutes and leave overnight in the pan, tightly covered. The next day, drain the wheat, which will have absorbed all the water and be tender enough to bite through. If the rice needs washing, wash and drain it in a colander for at least 30 minutes.

2. In a large, heavy saucepan with a well fitting lid, heat the butter and cook the onion, stirring, until it is golden. Add the cinnamon and drained rice, fry, stirring with a slotted metal spoon, for 5 minutes. Add the chicken stock, salt and pepper and the drained wheat. Bring to the boil, then turn the heat to low, cover tightly and cook for 20–25 minutes, until the stock has been completely absorbed. Do not lift the lid or stir during cooking time.

3. Uncover, allow the steam to escape for 5 minutes, then fluff the pilaf gently with a long-pronged fork. Meanwhile, melt the butter in a small frying pan and fry the slivered almonds until they are golden. Serve sprinkled with the slivered almonds.

—— **COOK'S TIP** ——

If not serving immediately, the pilaf may be reheated by steaming in a colander over simmering water.

STEAMED RICE

Perfectly cooked rice is not difficult to achieve, yet so many cooks shy away from it, convinced they cannot cook rice successfully. The secret lies in correct measures, low heat once it comes to the boil, and no peeking or stirring during the steaming. Rice lends itself to many variations, hot or cold, which are wonderful accompaniments to barbecued food.

Serves 6

500 g (1 lb) long grain rice
900 ml (1½ pts) water
1½ tsp salt
1 tbsp butter, optional

1. Wash the rice until the water runs clear then drain it in a colander for at least 30 minutes.
2. Put the rice, water, salt and butter, if using, into a heavy saucepan. Bring quickly to the boil, then cover the pan with a well fitting lid and turn the heat down very low. Cook for exactly 20 minutes, remove from the heat, uncover and allow the steam to escape for 5 minutes. Fluff the rice gently with a long-pronged fork.

ARROZ VERDE

Green rice – rice with fresh herbs – makes a good accompaniment to meat, fish or poultry. This is different to the dish of the same name as prepared in Mexico, and I prefer it done this way because it has more flavour and colour.

Serves 6

1 quantity steamed rice (see page 36)
50 g (2 oz) fresh basil leaves
125 ml (4 fl oz) olive oil
1 fresh green chilli, seeded and roughly chopped, optional
50 g (2 oz) pine nuts or walnuts
2 large garlic cloves
½ tsp salt
¼ tsp freshly ground black pepper
4 tbsp finely chopped parsley

1. While the rice is steaming, prepare the green sauce. Strip the basil leaves from their stems and put them into a food processor or electric blender with the olive oil and the chilli, if using. Blend to a purée, stopping the motor now and then to push the leaves down onto the blades. If necessary, add a little extra oil. Add the nuts, garlic, salt and pepper and blend again.
2. Leave the rice uncovered for 10 minutes after cooking has been completed, then turn it into a large bowl and pour the herb sauce over. Toss gently to mix and distribute the sauce, then sprinkle with the chopped parsley.

COOK'S TIP

When fresh basil is not available, make the sauce using parsley. Add a few sprigs of fresh thyme, oregano or marjoram or 2 tsp of dried herbs, for a more interesting flavour.

See photograph on page 117.

SPICED BASMATI PILAU

Basmati is a type of fragrant rice with thin, long grains which grow only in certain parts of India. It is undoubtedly the best rice for pilau (or pilaf) but it does need thorough washing and draining.

Serves 6

500 g (1 lb) basmati rice
3 tbsp ghee (clarified butter)
1 large onion, finely sliced
6 cardamom pods, bruised
1 quill of cinnamon
5 whole cloves
20 whole black peppercorns
½ tsp saffron strands
2 tbsp boiling water
900 ml (1½ pts) hot lamb or chicken stock
2 tsp salt

1. Wash the rice in several changes of water, and when the water runs clear, pour the rice into a large sieve and leave to drain, preferably for 1 hour.
2. In a large, heavy saucepan with a well fitting lid, heat the ghee and fry the onion and whole spices, stirring occasionally, until the onion is deep golden. Add the drained rice and fry, stirring with a slotted metal spoon, for 5 minutes.
3. Pound the saffron strands in a mortar with a pestle, add the boiling water and stir until dissolved. Add to the measured stock and pour it over the rice. Bring to the boil and stir in the salt. Cover the pan tightly and cook on the lowest possible heat for 20–25 minutes without lifting the lid or stirring. Uncover and allow the steam to escape for a few minutes. Lift out the whole spices which will be on top of the rice, and gently fluff with a long-pronged fork.

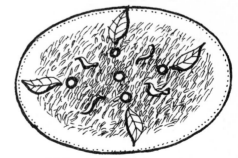

SERVING SUGGESTION

When dishing up rice use a metal spoon, as a wooden spoon will crush the grains. The pilau may be garnished as elaborately as you wish, with fried almonds, sultanas, cooked green peas, quartered hard boiled eggs, and, if you want to really make an impression, edible silver leaf. This is sold at some Indian groceries and is used for weddings or when entertaining someone important. But tell your guests what it is, or they may think you've overlooked the aluminium foil!

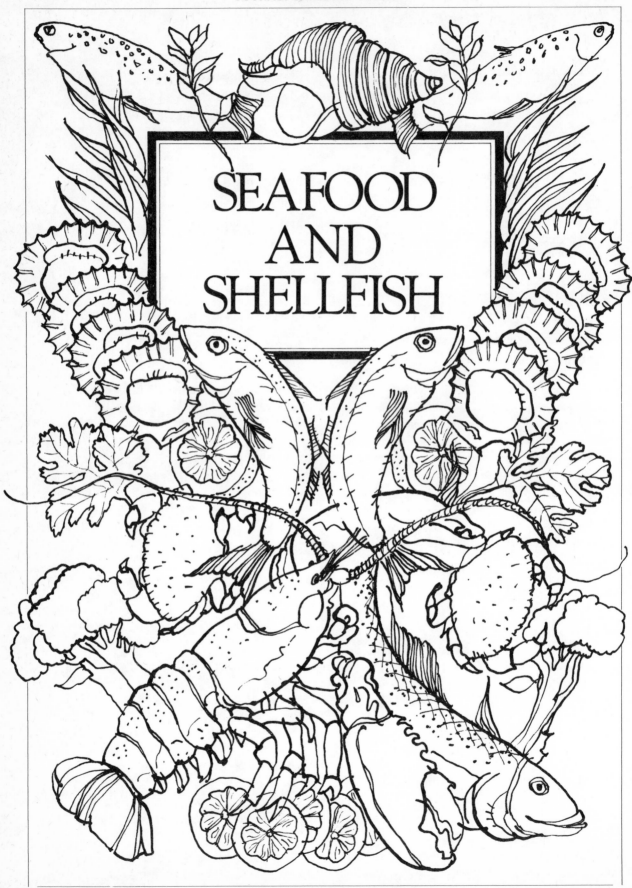

SEAFOOD AND SHELLFISH

Seafood on a barbecue is not new – remember reading about an early morning meeting on the shore of the Sea of Galilee, "a fire of coals there, and fish laid thereon . . ."?

In recent times, however, barbecues have come to convey a meaning that emphasises meat . . . regrettably, mostly burned. In this chapter I hope to enthuse all barbecue cooks about doing something rather different, and finding out how good seafood is when simply marinated and quickly cooked.

The most common fault in cooking seafood is that people are inclined to overcook it. I've been guilty of this myself, and must point out that it should never be left and ignored. Watch it carefully, because cooking times are not hard and fast. It all depends on how hot the fire is, how deep the bed of coals, distance of the grill or griddle plate from the source of heat, prevailing winds and a hundred other variables. So the watchword is . . . Watch it!

Stop fish cooking as soon as the flesh is firm and opaque. Remove prawns as soon as they become pink. Raw seafood is enjoyed in many parts of the world, so better to undercook it than have it dried out and tough.

Fish cooked in aluminium foil packages is wonderfully moist and flavoursome, but here again do check it earlier rather than later – it can always be replaced for further cooking, but what's done can't be undone. Wrapping in banana leaves is how people in the tropics often prepare fish for the barbecue, and if you live where this is possible, remember that the same rules apply – since you can't see what goes on inside the foil or banana leaf, check the cooking progress.

I particularly like using a fish-shaped wire basket for grilling whole fish – the fish is clearly visible, and may be tested at the thickest part (usually just below the head) by inserting the point of a knife. It is also easy to brush with marinade, and because it is double sided, it is easy to turn over with no danger of the fish breaking. Also, the hinges make it easy to remove the fish when done. To me, it is the best way to barbecue fish.

Barbecuing fish in a wire basket made for the purpose has been much more rewarding than my efforts at trying to cook a large fish on a rotating spit. When the fish cooks, the flesh flakes – naturally – and its hold on the spit becomes somewhat tenuous. However, if you do have a fish that is too large to fit into the basket, the way to prepare it for barbecuing is to pass a long metal skewer through its mouth and through the body to exit near the tail. This makes turning the fish easier.

Fish or shellfish kebabs, marinated and threaded on skewers, are particularly recommended, but do bear in mind that the grill must be oiled or the fish will stick.

In naming the kinds of fish I have used, I have also indicated what type of fish it is - firm, delicate, oily, and so on. This enables readers to use another local fish if the particular variety specified is not available.

As a general rule for barbecuing, use firm, thick fish steaks; fillets with the skin left on; or whole fish. If the choice is thin fillets or delicate fish, enclose them in foil or cook in a stout iron frying pan.

PUMPKINS WITH BÉCHAMEL PRAWNS

If you can find these one-serving size pumpkins, they look delightful and cook more quickly. If you have to use butternut or other larger varieties, allow longer cooking time and cut the pumpkins in half to make containers for the prawns.

For each person you will need:

1 small golden nugget pumpkin

4–6 large raw prawns, shelled and deveined

1 tbsp butter or oil

2 tbsp chopped parsley

2 tbsp chopped spring onion

salt and freshly ground black pepper, to taste

2 tbsp white wine

pinch of dried tarragon

125 ml (4 fl oz) béchamel sauce

Béchamel Sauce

250 ml (¼ pint) milk

slice of onion

fresh bay leaf and thyme leaves

freshly grated nutmeg

6 peppercorns

25 g (1 oz) butter

25 g (1 oz) flour

1. First make the sauce. Pour the milk into a pan, and add the onion, bay leaf, thyme, nutmeg and peppercorns. Bring to simmering point. Cover, remove from heat and leave to infuse.
2. Melt the butter in a small pan and stir in the flour. Cook, stirring, until straw coloured.
3. Gradually strain in the flavoured milk, stirring well between each addition. Season with salt and pepper and bring to the boil, stirring all the time. Cook 2–3 minutes until coating consistency is obtained. Cover and set aside until needed.
4. Cut off the top third of the pumpkins, and scoop and discard the seeds. Either steam or bake the pumpkins until just tender.
5. Heat the butter in a frying pan and sauté the prawns, parsley and spring onions until the prawns change colour. Transfer the prawns to the centre of the pumpkins, grinding a little salt

and pepper over to taste.
6. Put the white wine and tarragon into the frying pan and simmer until reduced by half. Add the béchamel sauce to the liquid and stir while heating through. Spoon the sauce over the prawns. The recipe may be prepared ahead up to this point.
7. Replace 'lids' on the pumpkins, wrap aluminium foil around the base, moulding it to shape, and place the pumpkins on the barbecue until heated through. Serve with a mixed salad.

COOK'S TIP

Scallops or chunks of a delicate fish may be used instead of prawns if preferred.

See photograph on page 25.

SIZZLING GARLIC PRAWNS

This would have to be the most popular dish in Spanish restaurants . . . it comes to the table in individual cast iron sizzle plates, the oil still bubbling, the prawns, garlic and touch of chilli giving off an unbelievably tempting aroma. Cook it over the barbecue using an iron frying pan which has the handle cast all in one with the pan, making sure you have an insulated pot holder to protect your hand. Serve with crusty bread which has been heated in aluminium foil until crisp.

Serves 6

1 kg (2½ lb) large raw prawns

125 ml (4 fl oz) olive oil

3 garlic cloves, crushed

¼ tsp Spanish saffron strands

1 tsp boiling water

1 fresh red chilli or dash of cayenne pepper

sea salt to taste

1. Shell the prawns, leaving just the last segment of shell next to the tail and the tail itself. This turns red when cooked.
2. Heat the olive oil in a heavy-based frying pan. Add the garlic and cook, stirring, until it is soft. Pound the saffron strands in a mortar with a pestle and dissolve in the boiling water. Stir in the saffron and chilli, and then add the prawns.

3. Turn the prawns over once or twice just until they turn pink, indicating they are cooked through. Do not overcook or they will be tough. If using cayenne pepper instead of chilli, add it now. Grind some sea salt over and toss the prawns through the well-flavoured oil, then serve with bread for taking up the juices.

SATAY PRAWNS

In Malaysia, Singapore and Indonesia, satays (small pieces of spicy marinated food on skewers, grilled over coals), are a way of life. People stop for a snack or a meal and the bill is calculated by the number of bamboo skewers left on the table.

Serves 4

700 g (1½ lb) raw prawns
3 tbsp lemon juice
3 tbsp thick coconut milk (see page 125)
1 tbsp soy sauce
1 tsp brown sugar
finely grated rind of 1 lemon
½ garlic clove, crushed
½ tsp salt
½ tsp sambal ulek (chilli paste)
½ tsp dried shrimp paste, optional
2 tbsp coconut milk or soy sauce
bamboo skewers, soaked for 1 hour

1. Shell and devein the prawns. Combine the lemon juice, coconut milk, soy sauce, sugar,

lemon rind, garlic, salt, sambal ulek and dried shrimp paste (if using) in a shallow bowl and marinate the prawns for at least 30 minutes. If leaving for a longer time, cover with cling film and refrigerate.
2. Thread 3 or 4 prawns onto each skewer and grill over glowing coals on an oiled grid.
3. Simmer the leftover marinade briefly, add the coconut milk and serve with the prawns as a dipping sauce. The usual accompaniment to satays of any kind is a compressed rice cake which is served cold, but a piece of crusty bread is very nice too.

TANDOORI-STYLE PRAWNS

This recipe was shared by a leading Indian restaurant specialising in *tandoor* (clay oven) cooking. It is also delicious cooked over a barbecue.

Serves 4

500 g (1 lb) large raw prawns
4 tbsp natural yoghurt
1 tbsp lemon juice
2 tbsp chopped fresh coriander leaves
1 tbsp chopped mint
1 garlic clove, crushed
1 tsp finely grated fresh ginger
1 tsp ground turmeric
1 tsp ground coriander
½ tsp chilli powder or to taste
wedge of lemon, to garnish
bamboo skewers, soaked for 1 hour

1. Shell the prawns, leaving only the last segment of shell and the tail on. Devein them, rinse and drain on kitchen paper.
2. Combine the yoghurt, lemon juice, coriander, mint, garlic, ginger, turmeric, ground coriander and chilli powder in a shallow dish, add the prawns and mix well. Cover with cling film and marinate for 20–30 minutes.
3. Thread the prawns onto 4 skewers and cook on an oiled grill for 3 minutes each side, turning the skewers so the prawns cook evenly. When they become opaque and the tails turn red, they are done. Serve on a small flat loaf, with lemon.

SUKIYAKI SCALLOPS

I like to cook marinated scallops quickly on a heated griddle. They take barely 2 minutes if the griddle is hot, so cook the vegetables until almost done and have accompanying rice or noodles ready before starting to cook scallops.

Serves 6

500 g (1 lb) scallops

| 3 tbsp sukiyaki sauce or Japanese soy sauce |

| 1 tsp grated fresh ginger |

| 1 tsp brown sugar |

| oil for cooking |

| 6 spring onions, cut into bite-sized pieces |

| 6 leaves of Chinese cabbage, cut into bite-sized pieces |

| 1 × 300 g (11 oz) can bamboo shoots, cut into bite-sized pieces |

1. Remove the dark vein from the scallops, wash quickly in cold water and drain thoroughly. Mix together the sauce, ginger and sugar in a bowl and marinate the scallops for at least 30 minutes.
2. When the griddle plate is very hot, pour 2 tbsp of oil onto the middle of the plate and spread with a wooden or metal spatula. Add the onions, cabbage and bamboo shoots and cook, turning them frequently, until they are tender but still crisp. Push to one side of the plate.
3. Heat another spoonful of oil on the plate and add the drained scallops. Cook, turning, until they are opaque and firm, but don't let them shrink and toughen. Serve immediately with the cooked vegetables. This is a good dish to eat with plain steamed rice.

ORIENTAL SCALLOP KEBABS

I think this is nicest cooked on a hot griddle plate, but if your barbecue doesn't have one, cook over the grill, basting, for a very short time.

Serves 4

500 g (1 lb) fresh scallops

| 3 tbsp soy sauce |

| 1 tbsp dry sherry |

| 2 tsp sugar |

| 1 tsp grated fresh ginger |

| 1 fresh hot chilli, seeded and sliced |

| 1 × 230 g (8 oz) can water chestnuts |

| 125 g (4½ oz) mange tout (snow peas), stringed |

| bamboo skewers, soaked for 1 hour |

1. Remove any dark veins from the scallops, wash briefly in cold water and drain thoroughly. In a bowl, combine the soy sauce, sherry, sugar, ginger and chilli, and marinate the scallops for 1 hour.
2. Thread the scallops alternating with the water chestnuts onto the bamboo skewers.
3. Cut the mange tout into julienne strips, then blanch them in boiling water for 1 minute and refresh in iced water. Drain and set aside.
4. Barbecue the skewered scallops until just firm, place on a serving plate and garnish with the mange tout.

— COOK'S TIP —
If mange tout are not in season, use very finely sliced French beans instead.

BURMESE FISH IN COCONUT MILK

In Burma, this would be wrapped in banana leaves but let's be practical and use aluminium foil. If you do have access to a banana tree, strip away the thick mid-rib of the leaf. Cut leaf into large pieces, then hold over heat to make pliable.

Serves 4

4 fillets of firm white fish
1 tsp sea salt
¼ tsp freshly ground black pepper
½ tsp turmeric
1 large and 1 small onion
2 garlic cloves, crushed
1 tsp chopped fresh ginger
1 fresh hot chilli or ¼ tsp chilli powder, optional
4 tbsp thick coconut milk (see page 125)
8 leaves of Chinese cabbage or cos lettuce, blanched and drained
2 tbsp ground rice or dry breadcrumbs
2 tsp Oriental sesame oil
1 bunch fresh coriander

1. Remove all skin from the fillets and cut each fillet in two. Grind the salt and pepper over them, sprinkle with turmeric and set aside.
2. Halve the large onion, slice it finely and reserve. Roughly chop the small onion and put it into the container of an electric blender or food processor with the garlic, ginger, chilli (if used) and coconut milk. Blend to a smooth purée. Pour over the fish pieces and mix well.
3. Place two cabbage leaves on 4 double pieces of aluminium foil or banana leaf. Put two pieces of fish on each cabbage leaf and spoon some of the sauce over. Sprinkle each portion with some of the ground rice and ½ tsp of sesame oil, the reserved, finely sliced onion and a few sprigs of the coriander. Wrap the fish first in the leaves and then bring the foil up and fold the edges into a seam at the top to make a package.
4. Place the packages on the barbecue and cook for about 8–10 minutes, depending on nearness to the heat and thickness of the fish. Serve an unopened package to each person. Hot steamed rice (see page 36) should be served with the fish, and try Cucumber and Sesame Relish (see page 112), also a Burmese favourite.

See photograph on page 45.

TUNA TERIYAKI

Fresh tuna is one of the delights of the deep. No wonder it is used so much in *sashimi*, the Japanese raw fish delicacy. It has no strong fish taste and lends itself to many marinades. But don't overcook it or it will become dry.

Serves 4

1 kg (2½ lb) fresh tuna or tunny fillet or steak
6 tbsp teriyaki sauce or Japanese soy sauce
3 tbsp mirin or dry sherry
2 tbsp sugar
2 tsp grated fresh ginger
½ tsp Oriental sesame oil
4 mild salad onions
corn or peanut oil for brushing
bamboo skewers, soaked for 1 hour

1. Using a very sharp stainless steel knife, trim all skin and dark coloured portions from the tuna. Cut the flesh into chunky pieces about 2.5 cm (1 inch) thick.
2. In a bowl, combine the teriyaki sauce, mirin, sugar, ginger and sesame oil, add the tuna and marinate for 1 hour.
3. Cut the onions into quarters, then into eighths crossways and separate into groups of two or three layers each. Thread alternate pieces of onion and tuna onto the bamboo skewers. Brush all over with oil.
4. Brush the grill with oil, place the skewers on it and barbecue just until the tuna turns pale pink and firm. Serve at once.

COCONUT FISH INDOCHINE

Originally devised as a tasty dish for a slimming gourmet, without the coconut milk.

Serves 4

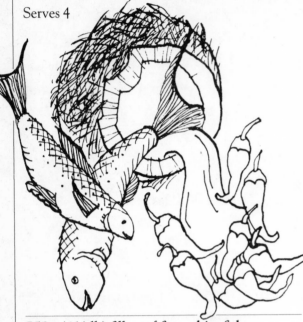

750 g (1½ lb) fillets of firm white fish

1 tsp chilli bean sauce or hot chilli sauce

2 tbsp coconut milk (see page 125)

2 tbsp tamari sauce or soy sauce

1 tbsp sherry

½ garlic clove, crushed

½ tsp grated ginger

½ tsp sesame oil

2 tbsp finely sliced spring onions

1. Place the fish fillets in a shallow dish. Make a mixture of the remaining ingredients and spoon it over the fish, turning the fillets until well coated. Leave for 15 minutes or longer.
2. Oil a grilling basket and place the fillets in it, or oil the barbecue grill and cook the fish over the coals for about 4 minutes on each side, depending on the thickness of the fillets. The fish looks milky white and opaque when done.

COOK'S TIP
The fish may also be cooked in aluminium foil parcels with the marinade spooned over.

CURRY-STYLE FISH KEBABS

Use a chunky type of fish for this recipe, leaving the skin on so it is easier to handle. The addition of ground rice to the marinade gives a touch of crispness.

Serves 6

1 kg (2½ lb) firm white fish fillets

1 garlic clove, crushed

2 tsp finely grated fresh ginger

1 tsp salt

1 tbsp ground coriander

1 tsp garam masala

½ tsp chilli powder, optional

250 ml (8 fl oz) natural yoghurt

good squeeze of lemon juice

1 tbsp ground rice

bamboo skewers, soaked for 1 hour

1. Wash the fillets, making sure all the scales have been removed. Dry well on kitchen paper. Cut the fillets into bite-sized pieces for threading on skewers.
2. Combine all the other ingredients in a bowl, add the fish pieces and turn them in the marinade until well coated. Leave for 15 minutes to 1 hour, then thread pieces of fish on the skewers, making sure all the skin is on one side of the skewer.
3. Put the skewers on a well oiled grill and cook 10 cm (4 inches) from the heat for about 4 minutes. Brush with a little marinade or oil, turn and cook the other side for 4–5 minutes, depending on the thickness of the fish. Serve hot with rice or flat bread.

Stuffed sardines with vine leaves (page 51); Burmese fish in coconut milk (page 43) with a Greek salad (page 92).

OVERLEAF
Left to right: Samaka harrah (page 50); Mexican fish steaks (page 50); Whole fish with ginger soy baste (page 53).

GOANESE FISH WITH GREEN HERBS AND COCONUT

This dish was served to me twice in the same trip to India, once in Bombay by descendants of the Persian settlers who came to India in the 13th century and once in Goa by descendents of the Portuguese.

Both dishes were essentially the same, yet tasted so different because the first one used very delicate white fish which was wrapped and cooked in banana leaves, while the Goanese version used robustly flavoured small mackerel and the fish was grilled over coals.

Serves 4

4 small whole fish or 750 g (1½ lb) fish fillets or steaks
coarse salt
1 large lime or lemon
2 medium onions, chopped
1 tsp finely chopped fresh ginger
1 garlic clove, crushed
2 large green chillies, seeded and sliced
small bunch fresh coriander or mint
1 tsp ground cumin
6 tbsp grated fresh coconut or desiccated coconut
1 tsp sugar
1 tsp salt
lime or lemon wedges, to garnish

1. Buy the fish gutted and cleaned but with the head left on. Scrub the body cavity with damp kitchen paper dipped in coarse salt then sprinkle the fish with salt and leave while preparing the coconut and herb mixture.
2. Peel the lime, removing all the white pith. With a sharp knife cut the fruit into sections, discard the seeds and put the flesh into the container of an electric blender or food processor. Add the onion, ginger, garlic, chillies and coriander. Blend on high speed until puréed. Add the cumin, coconut, sugar and salt, and blend again. It may be necessary to add a

tablespoon or so of water to facilitate blending, but the mixture should not be too liquid.
3. Coat each fish or fillet with the mixture and leave for at least 30 minutes. Wrap the fillets in aluminium foil and place on the barbecue. Whole fish can be cooked directly on the barbecue grill or in a fish basket until the skins have blistered and the flesh is opaque. Serve with wedges of lime or lemon.

JOHN DORY AND MANGE TOUT EN PAPILLOTE

Here's an elegant meal to plan when there aren't too many people to cook for. Very few barbecues have a griddle plate large enough to accommodate more than a couple of parchment paper parcels. However, they cook in such a short time that you could manage four, in relays.

Serves 2

2 × 185 g (6½ oz) fillets of John Dory or 4 smaller fillets
salt and freshly ground pepper, to taste
12 mange tout (snow peas)
2 tbsp ginger lemon butter (see page 54)

1. Wash and dry the fillets, season with salt and pepper. String the mange tout – preferably small, tender ones. If they are large, cut them into julienne strips.
2. On cooking parchment, place a dinner plate and trace the outline, then move it so it overlaps the first outline a little and trace another circle. Trace another outline and cut out the two shapes.
3. Place a fillet (or two if they are small) in the centre of one circle, put half the butter on top of the fish and strew half the mange tout over. Fold the parchment in half so the edges are together and fold the edges like a double hem, to seal the package well. Repeat with the remaining ingredients.
4. Have the griddle plate heated and ready; place the packages on it and barbecue on low heat. In a covered barbecue I find they are done in 5–6 minutes. Transfer the papillotes to plates for each person to open and enjoy the aroma. A hollandaise type sauce may be served with them.

Mango chicken with champagne (page 61) with Avocado and strawberry salad (page 93).

MEXICAN FISH STEAKS

I used Spanish mackerel which is a firm, quite strong-flavoured fish. Any firm fish cut into cutlets or steaks will do. Don't be alarmed at the amount of chilli, as long as you use Mexican chilli which is mixed with cumin, it is quite mild.

Serves 4

4 tbsp taco sauce

2 tbsp tomato sauce

1 tbsp chilli powder

4 medium-sized fish steaks, washed and dried

olive oil, for brushing

Mexican Chilli Sauce

2 tbsp olive oil

1 onion, finely chopped

1 garlic clove, crushed

1 red pepper or fresh hot chilli, seeded and chopped

3 medium-sized ripe tomatoes, peeled and seeded

20 pimiento-stuffed olives, sliced

2 tbsp chopped fresh coriander leaves

salt and freshly ground black pepper to taste

1. Make the sauce beforehand and have it ready. Heat the olive oil in a small saucepan and gently fry the onion, garlic and red pepper until soft. Add the peeled tomatoes and cook, covered, until they are soft and pulpy. Remove from the heat and reserve.
2. In a bowl, combine the taco and tomato sauces and chilli powder, add the fish, and marinate the steaks for about 15 minutes.

3. Drain the fish and reserve the marinade. Barbecue the fish over a well oiled grill or griddle, turning once and brushing with olive oil. It is cooked when the flesh is opaque and firm.
4. While the fish is cooking, reheat the sauce and stir in reserved marinade, sliced olives and coriander. Season to taste with salt and freshly ground pepper. Serve with the sauce and Arroz Verde (see page 37).

See photograph on page 46·47.

SAMAKA HARRAH

This is the way a good cook from Lebanon taught me to make stuffed grilled fish – very strong on garlic, so tone down that ingredient if you wish.

Serves 4

1 firm white fish, about 1 kg (2½ lb)

4 tbsp olive oil

1 large onion, finely chopped

1 carrot, finely chopped

1 red capsicum (pepper), finely chopped

1 or 2 hot red chillies, seeded and chopped

2 tbsp each fresh chopped parsley and coriander

3 or 4 garlic cloves, crushed

60 g (2½ oz) chopped walnuts

2 tbsp tahini (sesame paste)

lemon juice and salt, to taste

1. Ask the fishmonger to clean and scale the fish and remove the main bones as well, but to retain the shape of the fish. Clean out the cavity with damp kitchen paper dipped in coarse salt. Rinse and dry the fish.
2. Heat half the oil in a frying pan and sauté all the chopped vegetables, chilli, parsley and garlic (reserving 1 tsp) over low heat until they are soft, adding a little water now and then if necessary. Add half the walnuts and cook a few minutes longer, then purée the mixture in a blender or food processor to make a smooth sauce. Stir in the tahini and season to taste with lemon juice and salt.
3. Brush the fish inside and out with the remaining olive oil. Mix the remaining walnuts

with the reserved garlic, spread it inside the fish and wrap in a double layer of aluminium foil.

4. Grill the fish for about 8 minutes on each side. The fish may be grilled in a basket if preferred. Test by flaking the flesh with a fork and when opaque to the centre, it is done. Transfer to a platter and spoon the sauce over. Serve with pitta bread.

See photograph on page 46·47.

STUFFED SARDINES IN VINE LEAVES

It isn't as impossible as it sounds – sardines, anchovies and related bony fish must be cleaned and all bones removed if they are to be at all enjoyable, let alone edible.

First, remove the scales, then remove the heads and eviscerate the fish; a task made easier if you do it all through kitchen paper towels like I do. Wash the fish and pat dry.

Slip the point of a small, sharp knife between the flesh and the rib cage bones. Lift the backbone out from the head end and work it loose downwards without losing too much fish. Snip the bone when almost down to the tail, and you've got a fish with soft edible bones.

Serves 4

16 sardines or other small fish
2 tbsp olive oil
2 tbsp lemon juice
salt and freshly ground black pepper, to taste
32 vine leaves, fresh or brined

Stuffing

4 tbsp olive oil
1 large onion, finely chopped
2 garlic cloves, crushed
1 tbsp chopped fresh oregano or 1 tsp dried
2 tbsp finely chopped parsley
4 tbsp finely chopped walnuts
8 tbsp fresh white breadcrumbs
finely grated rind of 1 large lemon
good squeeze of lemon juice
sea salt and freshly ground black pepper

1. Prepare the sardines as described above. Mix together the olive oil, lemon juice, salt and pepper and marinate the fish in a shallow dish for 30 minutes.

2. Prepare the vine leaves for wrapping. If they are fresh, blanch them for a few seconds in boiling water to make them pliable. Brined leaves should be rinsed in warm water.

3. Combine all the ingredients for the stuffing in a bowl and mix well. Lay each sardine on a board, skin-side downwards and spread a spoonful of the stuffing over each fish, pressing it down firmly. Either roll the fish, starting from the head, or fold it together. In both methods the skin is on the outside.

4. Lay each fish on two vine leaves and wrap firmly. Barbecue over medium hot coals on an oiled grill. Small fish will only take about 2–3 minutes each side to cook, so watch carefully lest they dry out. Remove the vine leaves before eating the fish, and serve with Mixed Vegetable Medley (see page 24).

See photograph on page 45.

KOREAN GRILLADE

The flavours of a typical Korean marinade complement this not so well known *Gun Saengsun* just as well as they do the famous *Bulgalbi*, Korean barbecued beef.

Serves 4

4 small fish or 750 g (1½ lb) fillets
3 tbsp soy sauce
2 tsp sugar
3 tbsp toasted, crushed sesame seeds
1 tbsp Oriental sesame oil
1 garlic clove, crushed
1 tsp finely grated fresh ginger
½ tsp chilli sauce, optional

1. Buy the fish cleaned and scaled, with the heads removed. Trim the fins and tail and score each fish three times each side to allow the marinade to penetrate.

2. Combine all the remaining ingredients in a shallow bowl and marinate the fish for 15 minutes, coating in the marinade well. Cook on an oiled grill or in a fish basket over medium hot coals, brushing frequently with the marinade while cooking, to keep the fish moist.

GRILLED TROUT WITH SPRING ONIONS AND GINGER

This is a delicious way to cook trout, but I have also used a similar marinade on coarser, more economical fish such as trevally or cod and it does wonders.

Serves 4

---

4 serving size trout or 1 fish weighing 1 kg (2½ lb)

salt

½ tsp five-spice powder

2 tbsp peanut or salad oil

small bunch spring onions, bulb removed, finely shredded

3 tbsp finely shredded fresh ginger

2 tbsp soy sauce

2 tsp Oriental sesame oil

---

1. Wash the fish and clean the cavity thoroughly with kitchen paper dipped in salt. Rinse and dry. Make 3 or 4 shallow diagonal cuts in each side of the fish and rub well with a little salt and the five-spice powder.

2. Heat the oil in a frying pan and cook the spring onions and ginger until soft but not brown. Remove from the heat and add the soy sauce and sesame oil. Spoon some of the mixture into the cavity of each fish, and brush the remainder over the skin. Marinate for at least 15 minutes, then place the fish in a grilling basket and barbecue over medium heat until the skin has browned slightly. Flip the basket over and cook until the other side is also done. Serve at once.

SERVING SUGGESTION

Delicious though it is, there's not much to eat on a trout so serve these with Chinese Noodle Salad (see page 95) which is very much in character.

OTAK OTAK

I've visited Singapore more times than any other Asian country and it still fascinates me. Apart from the kaleidoscope of cultures, there is a wonderful array of food from all over the world. The taste I remember most vividly is that of an insignificant looking sliver of ground and grilled fish. It had been pressed within a strip of banana leaf and cooked over coals, and the flavour was stupendous. On a later visit I ate it again, this time slightly milder but still a force to be reckoned with.

Serves 4

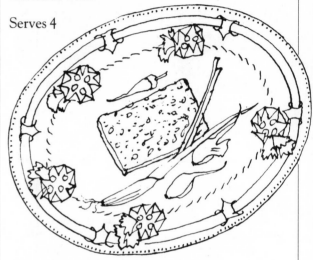

---

500 g (1 lb) fillets of firm white fish

3 dried red chillies

2 stems lemon grass or 4 strips lemon rind

2 garlic cloves

1 tsp salt

¼ tsp pepper

1 tsp sugar

2 tsp ground coriander

1 or 2 purple shallots, roughly chopped

4 candlenuts or 2 brazil nut kernels

½ tsp turmeric

2 tbsp chopped fresh coriander

1 fresh red chilli, optional

1 tbsp finely chopped Asian mint, optional

---

1. Remove any skin and bones from the fillets and chop very finely or purée in a blender or food processor.

2. Break the stems off the dried chillies and shake out and discard the seeds. Soak the chillies in hot water for 5 minutes. Use only the

tender white portion of the lemon grass and slice it finely.

3. Put the chillies, lemon grass, garlic, salt and pepper, sugar, coriander, shallots, candlenuts or brazils and turmeric in an electric blender or food processor and blend on high speed to form a smooth paste. Combine with the fish, mixing well. Stir in the chopped herbs.

4. Put 1 tbsp of the mixture onto double squares of aluminium foil and shape into small flat slices. Fold the foil over to seal the edges. Place the slices on the barbecue and cook for 4 or 5 minutes on each side. The fish turns opaque when cooked. Serve warm or cold. Good with salads such as Gado Gado (see page 96) or cucumbers in coconut milk.

WHOLE FISH WITH GINGER SOY BASTE

Give fish a subtle Oriental flavour and serve it with this dipping sauce based on the same ingredients.

Serves 6

1 whole coral trout or other delicate white fish
coarse salt
2 tbsp finely grated fresh ginger
2 tbsp Oriental sesame oil
2 tbsp soy sauce
4 tbsp orange juice or sherry

1. Ask the fishmonger to clean and scale the fish for you, then clean the cavity with damp kitchen paper dipped in coarse salt, removing all traces of blood. Rinse and dry the fish.

2. Combine the ginger, sesame oil and soy sauce and use half of it to rub the fish inside and out.

3. Add the orange juice to the remaining marinade and set aside to use as a dipping sauce.

4. Place the fish in an oiled grilling basket and barbecue over medium hot coals until golden brown on the underside. Turn the basket over and cook until the other side is also golden brown. Baste with the remaining marinade while cooking, adding a little water to it if necessary. The fish is cooked when it flakes easily at the thickest part and is white and opaque inside.

5. Transfer the fish to a serving plate and serve with the dipping sauce.

BARBECUED FISH WITH TARATOOR SAUCE

A favourite Lebanese way of serving fish – the tahini or sesame paste, which is a main ingredient, is sold in cans or jars at Greek or other Middle Eastern stores. Serve with Fattoush or Parsley and Cracked Wheat Salad.

Serves 4–6

1 whole firm white fish, about 1.6 kg (3½ lb)
salt
olive oil
25 g (1 oz) green and black olives, halved
finely chopped parsley, to garnish

Taratoor Sauce

1½ garlic cloves, crushed
1 tsp salt
8 tbsp tahini
6 tbsp lemon juice

1. Buy the fish cleaned and scaled, with the head left on. Wash well inside and out, then dry with kitchen paper. Rub well all over with salt, then rub generously inside and out with olive oil.

2. To make the sauce: In a mortar with a pestle, crush the garlic with the salt to a smooth paste. Add the tahini gradually and, little by little, beat in the lemon juice. If necessary, add a little water, to give the consistency of thick pouring cream.

3. Place the fish in a fish basket and grill over moderate coals, brushing frequently with olive oil, until the flesh is opaque and firm. Test by flaking the flesh with a sharp knife at the thickest part.

4. Lift the top off the basket and carefully remove the skin. Turn the fish over onto a large dish and remove skin from the other side. Spoon the sauce over, completely masking the fish, and garnish with halved or sliced green and black olives, and a sprinkling of parsley.

Alternatively, present the fish complete with skin and serve the sauce separately.

SNAPPER WITH GINGER-LEMON BUTTER

Any delicate-flavoured fish or shellfish, such as salmon steak, trout or lobster, would be suitable, and the flavoured butter doubles as marinade and sauce.

Serves 2

1 whole fish, about 500–750 g (1 lb–1½ lb) or 2 × 250 g (8 oz) fish fillets or steaks

salt and freshly ground pepper, to taste

90 g (3½ oz) butter, melted

1 tbsp finely grated fresh ginger

finely grated rind of 1 large lemon

2 tbsp lemon juice

1. Buy the fish cleaned and scaled, but with the head left on. Wash and dry the fish and slash the skin diagonally on either side. Rub with salt and pepper to taste.
2. Combine the butter, ginger and lemon rind, and use half the mixture to rub all over the fish, putting most of the ginger and lemon inside the cavity. Reserve some butter for brushing during cooking.
3. Add the lemon juice to the remaining butter mixture and set aside to serve as a sauce.
4. Place the fish in a wire grilling basket and barbecue over medium hot coals until the underside is done. Turn the basket over, brush with butter and continue to cook until the second side has browned. The fish is cooked when the flesh is firm and opaque. Serve immediately with the butter sauce, crusty bread and salad.

COOK'S TIP

If cooking a salmon steak or similar substitute, wrap the fish in aluminium foil. Since it would be placed directly on the barbecue, take care not to cook it for too long.

FISH WITH BACON AND TOMATO SAUCE

I prepared this using a small snapper, but any firm white fish such as bream would be suitable. If preferred, cook fillets instead of a whole fish and make separate parcels for easy cooking and serving.

Serves 4

1 whole fish, about 1 kg (2 lb) or 4 × 250 g (8 oz) fillets

salt and freshly ground black pepper, to taste

2 tbsp olive oil

2 onions, finely chopped

2 garlic cloves, crushed

4 rashers streaky bacon, rinded and finely chopped

3 large ripe tomatoes, diced

2 tbsp butter

2 slices white bread, crusts removed and diced

1. Clean and scale the fish and wipe out the cavity with kitchen paper dipped in salt. Rinse and dry the fish, then score the flesh on both sides and rub inside and out with salt and freshly ground pepper.
2. Heat the olive oil in a small saucepan and fry the onions and garlic until soft, then add the bacon and continue to fry until the bacon is cooked and the onions are golden. Add the diced tomatoes, cover and cook until soft. Add salt and pepper to taste, remove the pan from the heat and divide the tomato mixture into two equal portions.
3. Melt the butter in a frying pan and toss the diced bread until crisp. Mix the buttered crumbs into half of the tomato mixture and use it to fill the cavity of the fish. The recipe can be prepared ahead to this point.
4. If cooking a whole fish, take a large double thickness of aluminium foil and spoon some of the tomato mixture onto it. Place the fish on this and spoon the rest of the mixture over the fish. Place another piece of aluminium foil over the fish and fold the ends of both pieces together firmly, turning them over twice or more. This type of parcel enables the fish to be turned over during cooking. Barbecue for 8–10 minutes on each side until the flesh is opaque and firm. Serve accompanied by one of the flavoured breads (see page 101).

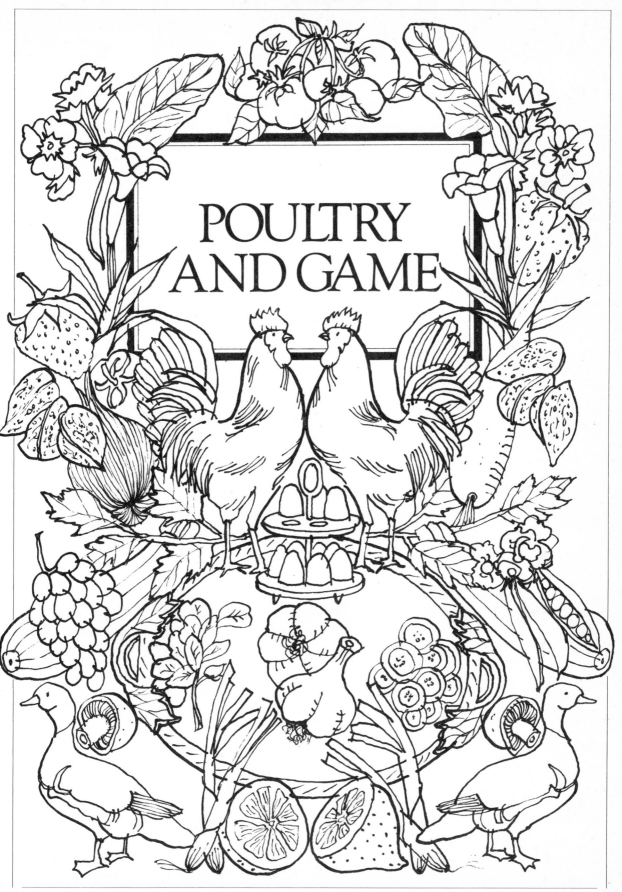

POULTRY AND GAME

As you read through the recipes in this chapter, you may wonder why I specify small chickens more often. It is for the simple reason that these cook better on a barbecue as the heat penetrates the not-too-thick flesh and presents a perfectly cooked bird rather than one which is overcooked outside and bloody near the bone.

Of course it is possible to cook a larger bird but keep a keen eye on the fire, make sure it is at a safe distance, and cook it slowly to ensure it has cooked through. It is much easier to cook a full sized roaster on a rotisserie. If you don't have one, cook the bird, turning it frequently. Either way, poultry needs brushing with marinade or oil. Take care that the oil or melting fat from the bird doesn't drip into the fire and cause flare-ups. Another trick that makes for more evenly cooked poultry is to cut the bird through the back with poultry shears, then flatten it. Thread it onto two metal skewers, one through the wings and another at the legs and base of the body, to ensure it *stays* flat.

Remove as much of the fat as possible (most of it is around the vent, tucked away beneath the skin). In some cases I have removed the skin altogether and covered the bird with a thick marinade. This gives a delicious result, as in the recipe for Tandoori-style Chilli Chicken (see page 61).

Chicken pieces are good for barbecuing because they are already portion-sized and the marinade has a better chance of penetrating the flesh. They cook in less time too.

ALMOND CHICKEN WITH CARDAMOM

Dreaming up recipes is a pleasure, and when putting it to the test endorses the choice of flavours, it is doubly rewarding.

Serves 4

| 2 chickens, about 600 g (1 lb 5 oz) each |
| 1 tbsp natural yoghurt or double cream |
| ½ tsp dried ground ginger |
| ¼ tsp salt |
| ¼ tsp white pepper |
| ⅛ tsp cardamom |

Stuffing

| 150 g (5 oz) whole grain breadcrumbs |
| 50 g (2 oz) almonds, roughly chopped and browned in 1 tbsp butter |
| ½ tsp ground cardamom |
| ½ tsp salt |
| freshly ground black pepper, to taste |
| 1 tbsp oil |
| 1 small onion, finely chopped |
| 2 tbsp garlic chives |
| 2 small eggs, beaten |

1. Wash the chickens inside and out and dry with kitchen paper. Mix the yoghurt with the spices and seasonings in a bowl and set aside.
2. To make the stuffing, combine the

breadcrumbs, almonds, cardamom, salt and pepper in a large bowl. Heat the oil in a frying pan and cook the onion and chives until soft but not brown. Add it to the breadcrumb mixture, then stir in enough beaten egg to moisten. Lightly pack the stuffing into the cavity of the birds and truss with poultry skewers.

3. Thread the chickens onto a spit and barbecue over medium heat until browned and crisp all over, brushing from time to time with a little vegetable oil.

4. When cooked, slide the chickens off the spit and cut each bird in two lengthways. Serve with Spiced Basmati Pilau (see page 37) as an accompaniment.

SPATCHCOCK WITH ORANGE MARINADE AND HAZELNUT STUFFING

This is one of the most delicious ideas I have come up with. I couldn't help thinking that here indeed is a gourmet barbecue meal which would make a romantic meal for two with plenty of flavour, but *NO* garlic. Instead of the pungent bulb, I offer you the refreshing fragrance of orange, the richness of toasted hazelnuts and a hint of sesame oil.

Serves 2

| 2 chickens, about 400 g (14 oz) each |
| 1 tsp finely grated fresh ginger |
| 1 tsp finely grated orange rind |
| 1 tsp sesame oil |
| 1 tbsp salad oil |
| 1 tsp dark sweet soy sauce (ketjap manis) |

Hazelnut Stuffing

| 80 g (3½ oz) hazelnuts, roasted and chopped |
| 80 g (3½ oz) fresh white breadcrumbs |
| ½ tsp finely grated orange rind |
| ½ tsp salt |
| ½ tsp white pepper |
| 2 tbsp butter |
| 2 spring onions, finely chopped |
| 1 tbsp currants |
| 2 tbsp beaten egg |

1. Wash and dry the chickens inside and out. Loosen the skin over the breast and front of the legs, laying the bird on its back and gently passing one hand between the flesh and skin. Combine the ginger, orange rind, oils and soy sauce, and rub it over the flesh. Marinate at room temperature for about 1 hour.

2. Meanwhile, combine the hazelnuts, breadcrumbs, orange rind, salt and pepper, and rub with your fingertips to distribute the flavours evenly.

3. Over gentle heat, melt the butter and cook the spring onions until soft but not brown. Stir into the hazelnut mixture with the currants and moisten with the beaten egg.

4. Divide the stuffing evenly between the chickens and fill the birds. Bring the neck flap over and fasten it with a small poultry skewer underneath the wings, which should be tucked under. Draw the body skin down and fasten it over the body cavity with another small skewer. Tie the legs together.

6. Thread the birds onto the spit and barbecue over medium heat for about 15–20 minutes (or longer for larger birds) or until they are a rich golden brown all over. Every 5 minutes, brush with the remaining marinade. Serve hot, accompanied by an orange and watercress salad.

—— COOK'S TIP ——
Roast hazelnuts in a moderate oven for 15 minutes. Wrap in a tea towel till cool, rub in the towel to remove skins.

HONEY SOY CHICKEN WINGS

Some modern barbecues have provision for cooking in a wok – that marvellously versatile Chinese cooking pan. But if your barbecue doesn't include this feature you can still enjoy the superb flavours of this recipe by starting the cooking in the kitchen and finishing it over coals.

Serves 6

1 kg (2 lb) chicken wings

2 tbsp peanut oil

1 garlic clove, crushed

1 tsp finely grated fresh ginger

4 tbsp dark soy sauce

2 tbsp honey

2 tbsp sherry

1 tbsp sweet chilli sauce (see page 110), optional

1. Cut the wings into separate joints. The wing tips are not used in this recipe but may be saved for stock.
2. Heat a wok or a large frying pan, pour in the oil and when it is very hot, fry the chicken wings over high heat until lightly browned. Add the garlic and ginger, and stir for a few seconds longer, then add the soy sauce, honey, sherry and chilli sauce. Stir well, turning the chicken wings over in the mixture.
3. Lower the heat, cover the pan and simmer for 25 minutes or until the chicken is tender. Take care that the sweet glaze does not burn, adding a little water if necessary. If starting the recipe indoors, simmer the chicken for 10 minutes only, then cool, and finish cooking on an oiled rack over glowing coals.

BARBECUED SAFFRON CHICKEN

The world's most expensive spice, saffron is not meant to be used lavishly, both for reasons of economy and because it can overpower other flavours. The strands (dried stamens of the saffron crocus) are the best way to buy this spice. If only powdered saffron is available, reduce the amount by half.

Serves 6

6 chicken thighs, skinned

1 medium-sized onion, roughly chopped

1 garlic clove, crushed

2 tsp finely grated fresh ginger

1 fresh red chilli, seeded and chopped

¼ tsp saffron strands

1 tbsp hot water

½ tsp ground cardamom

2 tsp salt

2 tbsp melted butter, to baste

1. To remove as much fat as possible from the chicken thighs, drop them into a saucepan of boiling water and when the water returns to the boil, simmer for 2 minutes. Lift out and allow to cool.
2. Put the onion into a food processor or blender with the garlic, ginger and the chilli. With mortar and pestle pound the saffron, then add the water and stir until dissolved. Pour into the blender with the cardamom and salt. Blend until smooth.
3. Make two slashes in each piece of chicken to allow the marinade to penetrate. Put the pieces in a flat dish and pour the marinade over, rubbing it into the slashes and over both sides well. Set aside for at least 2 hours.
4. If possible, thread the thighs onto skewers and cook, turning, about 10 cm (4 inches) from the heat, until the chicken is light brown and cooked through. Brush now and then with the melted butter. Serve warm, accompanied by Armenian Pilaf with Fruits (see page 93).

TANGERINE SMOKED CHICKEN

Fragrant and delicate, this dish is well worth the two-step cooking. Dried tangerine peel and star anise can be found in Chinese stores.

Serves 6

1 roasting chicken, about 1.5 kg (3 lb)
2 tbsp light soy sauce
2 tbsp Chinese wine or dry sherry
1 tsp salt
1 tsp sugar
4 slices fresh ginger, bruised
1 strip orange peel
2 spring onions

Smoking mixture

2 pieces dried tangerine peel
2 star anise
4 tbsp brown sugar

1. Rinse the chicken inside and out in cold water and wipe dry with kitchen paper. Combine the soy sauce, wine, salt and sugar, and brush it all over the chicken and inside the cavity. Leave for at least 30 minutes then brush again.
2. Put the slices of ginger, orange peel and the spring onions inside the chicken, then truss and tie the legs together. Place in a steamer and steam over boiling water for 15 minutes, then remove.
3. To make the smoking mixture, crush the tangerine peel and star anise as finely as possible in a mortar with a pestle, and mix with the brown sugar. Line an aluminium pan (or heavy cast iron pot) with heavy duty aluminium foil, bringing the foil up the side of the pan. Sprinkle the sugar mixture evenly over the foil.
4. Put a trivet or rack in the pan and place the chicken on it. If the pan has a well fitting lid, place it over the chicken or make a hood or tent of foil to keep the smoke in. If the barbecue has a lid, this will replace the foil tent. Place over low heat and allow the sugar and spice mixture to smoke the chicken for 20–30 minutes.
5. Serve the chicken warm or cold. It may be carved in joints or cut in half lengthways and then chopped with a heavy cleaver through the bones in the Chinese fashion. Serve accompanied by Chinese Noodle Salad (see page 95) or rice salad.

PACIFIC ISLAND PICNIC PARCELS

Pacific Islanders are always cooking outdoors, mostly in long shallow pits filled with stones which are brought to white heat. The food is wrapped in banana leaves or breadfruit leaves, and I once saw a whole pig being lifted from the imu (underground oven) in a large basket-like contraption woven of coconut leaves. So what if we don't intend to dig up our lawns, and if the average suburban garden doesn't yield banana, breadfruit or coconut leaves. Hurray for aluminium foil which brings us the joys of wrapping food with coconut milk and spices and cooking it on a barbecue. (If it rains, bring the parcels in and pop them in your oven – they taste just as good.)

Serves 4

1 kg (2 lb) chicken breasts or thighs
100 g (4 oz) creamed coconut
100 ml (4 fl oz) water
1 medium onion, roughly chopped
1 garlic clove
1 tsp turmeric
2 tsp salt
½ tsp freshly ground black pepper

1. If using chicken breasts, cut each into two. Trim excess fat from the thighs.
2. Gently heat the creamed coconut with the water, until dissolved. Pour into an electric blender or food processor with the onion, garlic, turmeric, salt and pepper. Blend until smooth. Alternatively, grate the onion finely and crush the garlic with the salt and mix it into the coconut mixture with the spices. Pour the marinade into a shallow dish and marinate the chicken pieces for 2 hours.
3. Make double thickness squares of aluminium foil large enough to enclose each piece of chicken and some marinade. Fold the foil together with a seam on top and barbecue the parcels for 25–30 minutes, keeping the seam on top so the juices don't run out. Serve with crusty bread to mop up the delicious sauce.

— COOK'S TIP —

If necessary, the parcels can be cooked for 45 minutes in an oven preheated to 180C, 350F, Mark 4.

MANGO CHICKEN WITH CHAMPAGNE

This is a dish you could serve with pride at any dinner party. It can either be cooked in a heavy frying pan from start to finish or, for a barbecue, browned and sautéed beforehand to ensure good flavour. You can use a roasting chicken, jointed, but I find that using chicken pieces (i.e. breasts, thighs, drumsticks) ensures more even cooking.

Serves 6

6 chicken pieces, breasts or thighs

3 tbsp plain flour

2 tsp salt

½ tsp freshly ground black pepper

4 tbsp ghee (clarified butter) or oil

3 large onions, finely sliced

2 firm ripe mangoes peeled and sliced or 1 large can mango slices, drained

200 ml (7 fl oz) champagne

6 tbsp double cream

1. Coat the chicken pieces in flour seasoned with the salt and pepper. Dust off any excess and fry the pieces in hot ghee until brown all over.
2. In the same frying pan, cook the onions over low heat, stirring, until they are soft and golden. If your frying pan is enamel or stainless steel continue, otherwise transfer the onions to a non-aluminium saucepan, add the champagne and simmer until reduced by two thirds.
3. Put the chicken pieces on large double squares of aluminium foil and divide the onion mixture among the parcels. Turn up the edges so the liquid doesn't run out.
4. Put the mango slices and 1 tbsp of cream in each parcel and add a good grinding of salt and pepper. Fold up the foil with the seam at the top to make a secure parcel, and cook over the barbecue for 30 minutes. Serve with crusty bread.

See photograph on page 48.

TANDOORI-STYLE CHILLI CHICKEN

A tandoor is an earthen oven in which food is lowered on very long metal skewers into intense heat. The marinade used here is the recipe given to me in Delhi by the chef of a five-star hotel. The cooking method has been adapted to suit the barbecue.

Serves 4

2 spring chickens, about 500 g (1 lb) each, skinned (except the wings)

200 ml (7 fl oz) natural yoghurt

1½ tsp salt

1½ garlic cloves, crushed

1½ tsp finely grated fresh ginger

½ tsp white pepper

½ tsp chilli powder

1 tsp garam masala

2 tsp paprika

1. Halve each chicken lengthways and make slits in the flesh to allow the flavour of the marinade to penetrate. Combine the yoghurt with the remaining ingredients and rub it all over and inside the chickens. Set aside for 2 hours at room temperature, or better still cover with cling film and refrigerate overnight.
2. Place the chicken halves, bone-side downwards, on the oiled grill or within an oiled grilling basket. Barbecue over hot coals, turning to cook both sides. If there is a rotating spit, leave the chickens whole, thread them on the spit and cook until tender and touched with brown on all sides. Serve half a warm chicken to each person and accompany with Naan (see page 100) or Wheat and Rice Pilau (see page 36) and finely sliced onions.

THAI GARLIC CHICKEN

When I used this in my first cookbook, a reviewer wrote that this recipe alone was worth the price of the book! I had better repeat here what I said then, that there is certainly a lot of garlic and pepper but the results are so delicious that I hesitate to modify the original. (Coarsely crushed peppercorns are not as hot as the same amount of finely ground pepper.)

Serves 6

6 thighs or half-breasts of chicken
6 garlic cloves
2 tsp salt
2 tbsp whole black peppercorns
4 whole bunches fresh coriander, or whole plants including roots, washed well
3 tbsp lemon juice

1. Remove any excess fat from the chicken, especially if using thighs.
2. Crush the garlic with the salt to make a smooth paste. Coarsely crush the peppercorns in a mortar with a pestle, or put them in a strong plastic bag and crush with a rolling pin. Finely chop the coriander herb, roots, stems and leaves. Add the lemon juice, mix all the seasonings together and rub into the chicken pieces well. Cover with cling film *and* aluminium foil and set aside for 1 hour or refrigerate overnight.
3. Barbecue the chicken over coals that have reached the steady glowing stage. Do not place too close, so the chicken cooks through. Turn the pieces every five minutes and finish by crisping the skin. Serve with boiled rice and tomato and onion salad.

CHICKEN SATAY

This Indonesian-style satay combines hot and sweet flavours. The marinade doubles as a sauce for dipping or spooning over.

Serves 6

750 g (1½ lb) chicken breasts
1 or 2 red chillies, seeded and roughly chopped or 1 tsp sambal ulek
2 medium-sized onions, roughly chopped
1 tbsp finely chopped fresh ginger
3 tbsp lemon juice
1 tsp salt
3 tbsp dark soy sauce
3 tbsp light soy sauce
2 tbsp sesame oil
2 tbsp dark brown sugar
6 tbsp thick coconut milk (see page 125)
bamboo skewers, soaked for 1 hour

1. Bone the chicken and remove the skin. Cut the flesh into bite-sized squares.
2. Put the chillies into a food processor or electric blender with the onions, ginger, lemon juice, salt and both soy sauces. Blend until smooth, then pour it into a shallow dish for marinating. Add the sesame oil and sugar, stirring until the sugar has dissolved. Coat the chicken pieces in the marinade well.
3. Cover the dish with cling film and marinate for 1 hour at room temperature or in the refrigerator overnight. Thread 4 or 5 pieces of chicken onto the pointed end of each skewer, leaving at least half the skewer free. Grill over glowing coals until the chicken is nicely

browned, turning and brushing with extra oil as necessary.

4. Pour the remaining marinade into a small saucepan, add the coconut milk and stir over low heat until smooth and thickened. Serve the satays with a small bowl of hot white rice with the sauce to pour over or dip into.

See the photograph on page 66·67.

TORI TERIYAKI

These morsels of grilled chicken in a flavoursome, yet delicate sauce, are very popular in Japan. Some versions include chicken livers, boned chicken pieces and lengths of spring onion grilled on skewers. Others call for the chicken to be on the bone.

Serves 4

4 half-breasts of chicken or 500 g (1 lb) chicken fillets and 250 g (8 oz) chicken livers

8 spring onions

4 tbsp Japanese soy sauce

4 tbsp mirin or dry sherry

1 tbsp sugar

1 tsp finely grated fresh ginger

½ tsp Oriental sesame oil

Dipping Sauce

3 tbsp soy sauce

3 tbsp mirin or dry sherry

3 tbsp chicken stock

bamboo skewers, soaked for 1 hour

1. Cut each half breast into two or three pieces. If using the boned chicken, cut it into 2.5 cm (1 inch) dice. Divide the chicken livers into bite-sized pieces, discarding any membranes and yellowish spots. Use both green and white portions of the spring onion and cut them into 5 cm (2 inch) lengths.

2. Mix the soy sauce, mirin, sugar, ginger and sesame oil together, stirring to dissolve the sugar. Marinate the chicken for as long as possible. Thread cubes of chicken and pieces of spring onion onto thin bamboo skewers, and the chicken livers on separate skewers, about 4 pieces to each skewer.

3. Meanwhile, combine all the ingredients for the Dipping Sauce in a bowl and reserve until required.

4. On the prepared barbecue, cook the pieces of chicken, bone-side downwards until cooked on that side, then brush with the marinade and cook the other side. Alternatively place the skewers on an oiled grill. Chicken livers will require about 4 minutes on each side or until firm and lightly browned. Skewered chicken needs only about 2 or 3 minutes. Chicken pieces on the bone will require longer, but be careful, do not overcook. Serve with the dipping sauce.

SERVING SUGGESTION

Another way of presenting this dish is to leave the breast whole and slash it crosswise at ½in. intervals, just deep enough to insert the lengths of spring onions. Thrust the skewer through the length of the breast.

See photograph on page 68.

TARRAGON POUSSINS WITH GOURMET MUSHROOM SAUCE

The fruitiness of wine and olive oil, the fragrance of tarragon and two kinds of mushrooms make this a special dish.

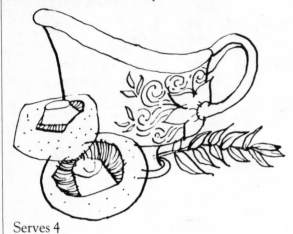

Serves 4

2 poussins about 500 g (1 lb) each

125 ml (4 fl oz) fruity white wine

1 tsp dried tarragon

1 tbsp olive oil

salt and freshly ground black pepper, to taste

watercress or parsley, to garnish

Mushroom Sauce & Stuffing

50 g (2 oz) dried cèpes

1 tbsp butter or oil

2 spring onions, including green tops, roughly chopped

150 g (5 oz) fresh mushrooms, roughly chopped

150 g (5 oz) fresh breadcrumbs, whole grain or white

4 tbsp cream

1. Wash the poussins inside and out and dry with kitchen paper. Remove any excess fat at the entrance to the body cavity, taking care not to damage the skin. Remove the necks if still attached. Very gently, slip your fingers between the skin and flesh around the neck and detach the skin from the body and legs, front and back. This allows the marinade to penetrate the flesh better. Proceed carefully as it is easy to tear the skin.

2. Put the wine and tarragon into a stainless steel or enamel saucepan and simmer until it has reduced to 2 tbsp. Transfer this to a shallow glass dish, add the olive oil and season with salt and pepper. Add the birds and marinate for 1 hour, spooning some of the herb-flavoured liquid into the cavity and between the skin and the flesh.

3. Put the dried cèpes into a pan with 250 ml (8 fl oz) water, bring to the boil, cover and leave for 10 minutes. Drain, reserving the liquid for the sauce. Chop the cèpes finely.

4. Heat the butter in a small saucepan and sauté the spring onions until soft but not brown. Add the cèpes and mushrooms and stir over low heat for a few minutes. Transfer half the mixture to a bowl, mix in the breadcrumbs and season to taste.

5. Stuff the birds with the mushroom and bread mixture, packing it loosely. Fasten the opening with poultry skewers and truss the poussins onto a spit. Barbecue over medium heat, either on a rotisserie or by turning frequently. Brush with the marinade from time to time until the birds are golden brown and crisp all over. Transfer to a chopping board, halve lengthways and arrange on serving plates, cut side down.

6. Add the soaking liquid to the mushrooms remaining in the pan, discarding any sediment at the bottom. Cook, uncovered until the sauce has reduced or thicken it slightly with 2 tsp of cornflour mixed smoothly with 1 tbsp of cold water. Add the cream and heat through, stirring. Pour over each portion of poussin. Garnish with a sprig of watercress and serve with a green bean and walnut salad.

Oriental-style pork fillet (page 85) with Chinese noodle salad (page 95).

OVERLEAF
Chicken satay (page 62); Souvlakia (page 79); Singapore-style pork satay (page 84); Beef and coconut fricadelles (page 82) with Gado gado (page 96) and Indonesian peanut sauce (page 110).

HERBED CHICKEN WITH WALNUT SAUCE

Make sure the walnuts are fresh – otherwise the flavour of walnut oil may be overpowering in this delicious sauce.

Serves 4

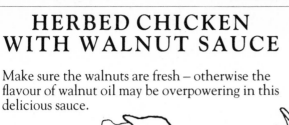

2 roasting chickens, about 1 kg (2 lb)

juice of 2 lemons

6 tbsp olive oil

1 garlic clove, crushed

1 tsp salt

generous grinding of black pepper

2 tbsp chopped fresh oregano

1 tbsp chopped fresh thyme

Spiced Walnut Sauce

175 g (6 oz) very fresh walnut kernels

50 g (2 oz) fresh white breadcrumbs

250 ml (8 fl oz) chicken stock

1 onion, finely chopped

1 garlic clove

1 tsp paprika

½ tsp salt or to taste

freshly ground black pepper, to taste

2 tbsp lemon juice

finely chopped parsley

extra paprika for garnish

1. With poultry shears, cut the chickens into 4 portions each. Cut off and discard the wing tips and tail. Each person will have a half breast and wing, thigh and drumstick.
2. Combine the remaining ingredients in a shallow dish to make a marinade. Add the chicken, turning each piece in the mixture until well coated. Set aside for at least 2 hours. Meanwhile, make the sauce. Put the walnuts, breadcrumbs, stock, onion, garlic and paprika into blender and blend until smooth. Season to taste.
3. When the barbecue is at the right stage for grilling, oil the grid or, better still, two grilling baskets. Drain off the marinade so it doesn't drip onto the coals.
4. Put the thigh and leg pieces in one basket, the breasts in another, as they need different cooking times. Barbecue the thighs and drumsticks for 15 minutes, so start them first. Five minutes later, add the breasts and cook for 10 minutes, watching them carefully to ensure they don't dry out. Turn the pieces and brush with marinade as required.
5. As soon as the skin has browned, transfer them to a serving plate and spoon the Walnut Sauce over each piece. Sprinkle with parsley and paprika and serve with Wheat and Rice Pilau (see page 36) and a green salad.

Top: Marinated Japanese beef with spring onions (page 81) and Tori Teriyaki (page 63).

COOK'S TIP

If fresh herbs are unavailable, use dried herbs, reducing the quantity to one quarter of that suggested for fresh herbs.

TANDOORI-STYLE CHICKEN KEBABS

While travelling through India to research a book on regional food, I was served this delicious version of *Tikka Kebab* in a tandoori restaurant. The chef was generous enough to share the recipe.

Serves 4–6

1 kg (2 lb) chicken thighs, skinned and boned
1 onion, roughly chopped
1 garlic clove, crushed
1 tsp chopped fresh ginger
1 tbsp lemon juice
2 tbsp natural yoghurt
1 tsp ground coriander
1 tsp ground cumin
1 tsp garam masala
1 tsp salt
1 tbsp ground almonds or white poppy seeds

1. Cut the chicken meat into 2.5 cm (1 inch) pieces. Put the onion, garlic, ginger and lemon juice into a food processor or blender and blend until smooth. Mix in the remaining ingredients and marinate the chicken pieces for at least 2 hours, or overnight in the refrigerator.
2. Thread the chicken onto metal skewers, or onto pre-soaked bamboo skewers and grill over glowing coals, turning them frequently so that the chicken has browned lightly on all sides. Serve with finely sliced raw onion and either Wheat and Rice Pilau or Naan bread (see pages 36 and 100).

CHICKEN POZHARSKI

There are a few famous Russian ways of cooking chicken, perhaps the best known being *Chicken Kiev*. This is another, *Pozharski Cutlets*, and while Kiev doesn't translate to a barbecue situation, these do well on a griddle plate or in a heavy iron pan.

Serves 6

1 kg (2 lb) chicken thighs, boned
6 slices white bread, crusts removed
5 or 6 tbsp milk
1 onion, finely grated
1 tsp salt
½ tsp white pepper
2 tbsp melted butter
2 tbsp finely chopped parsley
1 tbsp finely snipped chives
1 tbsp snipped fresh dill
dry breadcrumbs, for coating
3 tbsp ghee (clarified butter), for frying

1. Remove the skin and chop the chicken meat finely or put through a mincer, using the coarse screen.
2. Cut the bread into small dice and put into a bowl. Pour the milk over and when the bread is soft, mix it with the chicken, then put both through the mincer. Mix in the onion, salt, pepper, melted butter and herbs.

3. Form the mixture into thick hamburger shapes. Coat them in the dry breadcrumbs and refrigerate.

4. Heat the griddle plate or large frying pan and melt a little of the ghee. Add the cutlets, not crowding them, and barbecue over medium heat until the underside is golden brown. Turn and cook the other side in the same way, adding more ghee as necessary. Serve warm, garnished with parsley sprigs and accompanied by a Russian Salad (see page 92).

ORIENTAL BARBECUED DUCKLING

If it rains and spoils your plans for a barbecue, console yourself if duck is on the menu with the thought that duck is more tender and juicy if cooked in an oven and preferably in an oven bag. But of course that won't give you that wonderful barbecued flavour. Here are a couple of hints to help you get the best results . . . like a quick turn in the oven first to rid the duck of excess fat.

Serves 4

1 roasting duckling, about 2 kg (4 lb)
1 garlic clove, crushed
1 tsp finely grated fresh ginger
1 tsp sesame oil
1 tbsp honey
1 tbsp soy sauce
1 tsp salt
½ tsp freshly ground black pepper

Garnish and Accompaniment

4 firm, ripe tamarillos
4 tbsp sugar
8 tbsp water

1. Remove the neck and giblets from the duck and use for stock. Wash the duck inside and out and dry with kitchen paper. Put the duck, breast downwards on a rack in a roasting tin and prick all over to let the fat run. Roast in a preheated oven at 230C, 450F, Mark 8 for 20 minutes. Turn the bird over and continue roasting for a further 15 minutes. Remove from the oven and leave until cool enough to handle.

2. Combine all the remaining ingredients to make the marinade. Tilt the duck so any liquid collected in the body cavity runs out. Apply some of the marinade to the inside of the cavity and, if liked, place a couple of spring onions inside. Rub the duck all over with the rest of the marinade, cover and leave for about 4 hours or overnight if possible.

3. Meanwhile, make the garnish; pour boiling water over the tamarillos and after 1 minute, plunge them into cold water. Peel away the skin, leaving the stem. With a sharp knife, cut 3 or 4 slices from the bottom almost to the stem of each fruit. Put the sugar and water into a saucepan and heat until the sugar has dissolved. Poach the tamarillos gently in the sugar syrup for about 7 minutes or until tender, but still holding their shape. Reserve.

4. Thread the duck onto the spit of a rotisserie and cook over low heat on a covered barbecue. Have the spit at a respectful distance from the coals and cook, turning, for at least 1 hour or until the skin is deep golden brown and the juices run clear when a fine skewer is inserted into the thigh. If the juices are pink, the duck needs longer cooking.

5. Remove the reserved tamarillo slices from the pan with a slotted spoon and arrange in a fan shape on each plate. When the duck is ready, slip it off the skewer, cut it into portions and put onto the serving plates.

INDONESIAN SPICED QUAIL

Once, at a Vietnamese restaurant, we were served the most delicious dish of quails which had been marinated in a mixture of sauces and spices. The marinade may be used on small chickens too. Split them down the back and open out flat, or halve them lengthways and cook in the same way.

Serves 6

6 dressed quail
2 tbsp Vietnamese fish sauce
2 tbsp rice wine or dry sherry
1 tbsp light soy sauce
1 garlic clove, crushed
1 tsp finely grated fresh ginger
½ tsp freshly ground black pepper
½ tsp five-spice powder
1 tsp hoi sin sauce
vegetable oil for brushing

1. Cut the quails in half lengthways, and wipe out the body cavity with kitchen paper and dry them well. Combine the fish sauce, rice wine, soy sauce, garlic, ginger, pepper, five-spice powder and hoi sin sauce in a shallow bowl. Marinate the quails in the mixture for at least 4 hours or overnight in the refrigerator covered with cling film.
2. Place the birds on a well oiled grill, skin-side upwards, and cook until done on one side. Brush the skin with the oil then turn the pieces over with tongs and cook on the other side, not too close to the heat.
3. When the skin is brown and crisp, transfer the birds to a warm dish and serve with a salad or with moulded mushroom rice for heartier appetites.

RAJASTHANI-STYLE QUAIL

I have named this recipe after the area in India where I had the experience of being entertained at a Maharaja's hunting lodge, and watched peacocks and wild game emerge from the forests at sunset. This marinade goes equally well with chicken, but chicken legs or quarters are more suitable than a whole bird.

Serves 2–4

4 dressed quail, about 150 g (5 oz) each
1 garlic clove, crushed
1 tsp finely grated fresh ginger
1 tbsp oil
1 tbsp water
2 tsp ground rice
2 tsp ground coriander
1 tsp ground cumin
1 tsp ground turmeric
½ tsp salt
½ tsp freshly ground pepper
¼ tsp chilli powder, optional

1. With poultry shears, cut the quail down the back and open out flat. Clean out the cavity with folded kitchen paper, rinse each one in cold water and blot dry.
2. Combine the remaining ingredients for the marinade and rub it generously over the quail on both sides. Cover with cling film and marinate at room temperature for 1 hour or longer in the refrigerator.
3. Thread two skewers through each bird, one at the neck and wings and the other at the legs, to keep them flat while cooking. Grill for about 8 minutes, turning and brushing once or twice with the remaining marinade, mixed with 1 tbsp of oil and water. Cook the quail until brown and crisp (the ground rice gives a nice crunchy coating) and serve with Spiced Basmati Pilau and Cucumbers with Soured Cream (see pages 37, 98).

See photograph on page 117.

MEAT

Let me tell your about barbecuing and the wide ranging effect it has on everything, including the weather! Why am I springing this on you in the middle of the book, and as a prelude to the chapter on barbecuing meat?

It just so happens that very recently I visited friends in the country, this big, sunburnt country, Australia, where every drop of rain is a blessing. They grow wheat, barley, sheep and other crops too, but at this time the barley and wheat were at the stage where good, soaking rain was needed to save the crop. As we drove around the 3000 acres the sky was brilliantly blue, the day warm.

They had planned to spit roast a whole lamb that night, and the barbecue was set up, together with the spit and the mechanism which would keep the beast turning over the coals. All excess fat trimmed away, it had been threaded on the spit and stored in the cool room . . . a necessity on an Australian farm.

Ever seen a sheep in a shower? No, I don't mean those outdoor contraptions where live sheep are soaked with sheep dip. I mean a sheep in a shower recess normally used by people. Bet you haven't, and neither had I, until then. But it made good sense, to run hot water over it until the temperature of the carcass was raised by several degrees ensuring it would take less time to cook.

The fire was started, the beast loaded on the supports and the motor switched on. It didn't take too long for the skies to cloud over and a brisk wind started up. Prepared for everything, the men erected sheets of metal which formed a sort of outdoor oven around the lamb. Valiantly they kept going, but all too soon there was a downpour and all the would-be cooks had to run for the shelter of the house. The electric rotisserie was turned off and the women started to hurry with the alternative menu.

Pasta salad with freshwater crayfish (yabbies) from their own dam: cold chicken which had been boned, filled with a meaty dressing and roasted; young, tender sugar snap peas and mange tout (snow peas) from the vegetable garden and Gado Gado (cooked vegetables served Indonesian style with a peanut sauce). There was no shortage of good things to eat, but we all kept thinking about the half-cooked lamb outside.

As suddenly as it started, the wind dropped and the rain dwindled to a few drops. Out we went again, wrapped the electrical connections in plastic and started the barbecue fire and rotisserie once more. To hurry things up, they also lowered the spit so it was nearer the fire.

It was not until some time later that one of the youths discovered that the spit had slipped and the lamb, instead of turning, was just sitting there. Moreover the fat, dripping onto the coals, had started a nice little blaze, with the choice rib portions burning away merrily. Someone dashed off for the water spray and doused the flames, and by this time the fellows were determined to taste the lamb, burnt offering or no.

The more restrained among us waited until more meat had cooked, and it was sliced and brought to the table. We heard later that those portions, sliced and eaten straight off the spit, were the most delicious of all!

I tell this story to emphasise the wisdom of always having an Alternative Plan, so all the recipes in this chapter are eminently suitable for cooking under a grill, or in the oven.

SPIT-ROASTED LAMB WITH HERBS

In a country like Australia it is quite common for barbecues to include a whole lamb, pig or steer roasted on a spit. There is plenty of time for swapping yarns and socialising while the electrically operated spit turns the beast over the coals. Even when barbecues are gas-fired, they feature a layer of volcanic rock and sometimes this is added to with chips of hickory wood, prunings of fruit wood, and perhaps a few gum leaves for that outback flavour. The following recipe was given to me by the chef at the Argyle Tavern, in one of Sydney's historic buildings, where spit roasting a steer or a lamb is a feature.

Serves 30

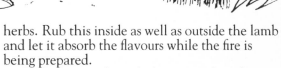

1 lamb, about 15 kg (30 lb)
salt and freshly ground black pepper, to taste
4 garlic cloves, crushed
8 tbsp olive oil
2 tbsp dried oregano
2 tbsp dried rosemary
bunch of fresh rosemary and oregano sprigs

1. The lamb requires about 3 hours to cook. About 2 hours before cooking starts, light the fire to create a good bed of coals. If a gas barbecue is used, light it 15 minutes beforehand to heat the volcanic rock.
2. Ask your butcher to prepare the lamb for spit roasting, but there are a few things that will be up to the chef. Firstly, make four cuts in the lamb's shoulders and legs where the meat is thickest. Place tightly rolled aluminium foil in these cuts to act as a heat conductor and aid even cooking.
3. Season the lamb well with salt and pepper, inside the body cavity and all over the outer surface. Combine the garlic, olive oil and dried herbs. Rub this inside as well as outside the lamb and let it absorb the flavours while the fire is being prepared.
4. Push the spit through the carcass lengthwise and secure with skewers provided. For additional anchorage, wire the carcass to the spit with chicken or picture wire. The chef prefers to wrap the lamb in several layers of heavy-duty aluminium foil for less shrinkage. All the juices are sealed in and the meat cooks evenly. My country friends prefer not to foil-wrap the lamb, they like the flavour it derives from the open cooking. I recommend wrapping only the rib portion where the meat is not very thick, and unwrapping it just before the heavier joints are done, to brown and crisp the surface.
5. Place the spit over the bed of coals and cook for about 2½–3 hours, stoking the fire without creating flames. At the end of cooking time, remove the lamb from the spit, release the wire and leave for half an hour to allow the juices to settle back into the meat. Carve and serve with piquant sauces or mint jelly. An Armenian Pilaf with Fruits (see page 93) would be an ideal accompaniment.

SMOKED BUTTERFLY LEG OF LAMB

This method of preparing the leg of lamb presents more surface area, the better to capture the flavour of hickory smoke. If preferred, use a simple marinade of olive oil, lemon juice and herbs.

Serves 6–8

1 leg of lamb, about 2 kg (4 lb)
2 tsp finely grated fresh ginger
1 garlic clove, crushed
½ tsp salt
½ tsp freshly ground black pepper
1 tsp turmeric
2 tsp ground coriander
2 tsp ground cumin
3 tbsp light soy sauce
1 tbsp ground rice
2 tsp sesame oil

1. Ask the butcher to butterfly the leg of lamb, that is, to bone it and open it out flat. You can do this yourself with a sharp knife, working from underneath where the bone is very close to the surface. Keep the knife close to the bone so that no meat is wasted. Carefully trim off excess fat and the covering membrane in places where it is very thick. Remove nuggets of internal fat too.
2. Combine the remaining ingredients for the marinade and rub into the lamb well. Cover with cling film and leave for at least 1 hour.
3. Pass the rotisserie spit or two long skewers through the lamb, 'stitching' in any straggling pieces of meat, or fasten these neatly with poultry skewers. If the rotisserie is being used, push the prongs in place and make sure the meat is balanced.
4. Prepare the barbecue fire and when the coals are glowing, add a handful of hickory chips which have been soaked in water for at least an hour. Set the meat rotating on the spit, ensuring it is not too close to the heat, and put the cover of the barbecue in place. It is possible to fashion a makeshift cover with wire and aluminium foil, but nowadays most barbecues offer the option of a cover which is most useful as a windbreak or when smoking the food.
5. On low heat the leg of lamb should take 40–50 minutes. Around the edge of the barbecue I would cook thick slices of butternut pumpkin and onion wrapped in foil.

KASHMIRI-STYLE LAMB

Plan ahead for this, because the longer it is marinated, the better the flavour.

Serves 8

1 leg of lamb, about 2.5 kg (5 lb), boned
1 tbsp finely grated fresh ginger
2 garlic cloves, crushed
2 tsp salt
1 tsp ground cumin
1 tsp ground turmeric
½ tsp ground cinnamon
½ tsp ground cardamom
½ tsp freshly ground black pepper
¼ tsp ground cloves
3 tbsp lemon juice
½ tsp saffron strands or ¼ tsp powdered saffron
½ cup thick natural yoghurt
2 tbsp blanched almonds
2 tbsp pistachio kernels
1 tbsp honey

1. With a sharp knife, trim the excess fat off the lamb and make deep slits all over. Place the

lamb in a dish in which it can be stored in the refrigerator.

2. Combine the ginger, garlic, salt, all the ground spices and lemon juice, and rub this mixture into the lamb well, pressing it into each slit.

3. If using saffron strands, pound them in a mortar with a pestle, then dissolve them in 2 tbsp of boiling water. Stir it into the yoghurt. Pound the almonds and pistachio kernels to a paste or grind in a blender. Mix with the yoghurt and spoon it over the lamb and in the hollow where the bone has been removed. Drizzle the honey over. Cover with cling film and marinate at least overnight, longer if possible.

4. When ready to barbecue, wrap the lamb in a double thickness of aluminium foil, sealing it well so the juices cannot be lost. Cook over coals that have reached the glowing stage, or not too close to the source of heat. Allow 1 hour per kilo (2 lb) cooking time. When cooked, allow the meat to rest for at least 30 minutes before carving. Serve with some of the spicy marinade and accompanied by Steamed Rice or Naan bread (see pages 36 and 100).

SHASHLYK

I first tried this famous dish on a Russian ship and the cubes of lamb were presented on skewers long enough to be used as swords, which were propped up against each other in a pyramid, a red tomato on the point of each. They were served with flat Georgian-type bread and spring onions, and I was given the recipe by the Chief Catering Officer.

Serves 6

| 1 leg of lamb, about 2 kg (4 lb), boned |
| 250 ml (8 fl oz) dry white wine |
| 1 tbsp olive oil |
| 1½ tsp salt |
| ½ tsp freshly ground black pepper |
| 1 small onion, finely grated |
| 1 lemon, cut into eighths |
| spring onions and lemon wedges, to garnish |

1. Trim all excess fat off the lamb and cut away the bottom third to use in another dish, such as Seekh Kebab (see page 79). Use only the

choicest portions for this dish and cut the meat into large cubes.

2. Combine the wine, olive oil, salt, pepper and onion in a large shallow bowl. Remove the pips from the lemon and squeeze the juice into the mixture, then drop in the lemon skins for added flavour.

3. Add the lamb cubes to the marinade and mix well. Leave at room temperature for 4 hours or cover with cling film and refrigerate overnight.

4. Thread cubes of lamb onto long metal skewers and barbecue over steadily glowing coals, turning the skewers and brushing with the marinade until the lamb has browned on all sides. Do not place the meat too close to the heat, because Shashlyk should be well done. Serve hot, with pitta bread or pilaf and garnished with spring onions and lemon wedges.

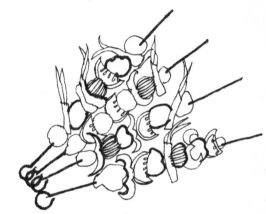

SERVING SUGGESTION

If liked, the cubes of lamb may be alternated with sections of spring onion, wedges of tomato and pieces of green capsicum (pepper) or courgette (zucchini), and a cherry tomato placed on the tip of each skewer for serving. Good-quality beef can be substituted for the lamb.

LAMB CHOPS WITH ROSEMARY MARINADE

Use fresh, tender rosemary leaves for this marinade. I prefer raspberry vinegar but any good red wine vinegar may be used instead.

Serves 6

6 large lean forequarter lamb chops

3 tbsp raspberry or red wine vinegar

6 tbsp olive oil

1 tbsp finely chopped fresh rosemary

2 garlic cloves, crushed

1 tsp salt

½ tsp freshly ground black pepper

1. Trim any fat off the chops and snip the edges to prevent them curling.
2. Whisk the vinegar and oil together, then add the remaining ingredients and mix until thoroughly combined. Put the lamb chops in a large, shallow dish and pour the marinade over, turning them to coat both sides. Cover with cling film and leave overnight in the refrigerator or at room temperature for at least 2 hours.
3. Grill over high heat to seal both sides, then move the rack further away from the coals, or turn down the heat and continue cooking until done to taste, basting occasionally with the remaining marinade. Serve hot with a relish such as Spiced Prunes (see page 112).

BEST-EVER SPICED LAMB KEBABS

There is no use pretending this is a classic recipe, I made it up and have never regretted it. Our favourite – and that goes for our guests too.

Serves 6–8

1 leg of lamb, about 2 kg (4 lb), boned

1 garlic clove, crushed

2 tsp salt

2 tsp finely grated fresh ginger

1 tsp freshly ground black pepper

1 tsp ground turmeric

1 tsp ground coriander

1 tsp ground cumin

1 tsp crushed dried curry leaves

1 tsp crushed dried oregano leaves

1 tbsp light soy sauce

1 tbsp Oriental sesame oil

2 tbsp peanut (groundnut) oil

1 tbsp lemon juice

1. Trim excess fat off the lamb, and remove the sinewy lower portion of leg, which can be used in another dish. Cut the meat into 2.5 cm (1 inch) cubes and put into a large bowl. Combine the remaining ingredients to make the

marinade, then pour it over the lamb and mix well. Make sure every cube of lamb is covered with the marinade.

2. Cover the bowl with cling film or aluminium foil and refrigerate for at least 4 hours, preferably a whole day or more.

3. Thread 4 or 5 pieces of meat onto each skewer and barbecue over a steady heat, turning every 2 or 3 minutes, until the cubes are nicely browned and sizzling. Because of the oil in this marinade, it is seldom necessary to brush the lamb while cooking. Serve hot with rice or pitta bread and onion sambal.

COOK'S TIP

Dried curry leaves are easily found at Indian groceries, but you have to crush them yourself. I use an electric blender.

SEEKH KEBAB

When you trim the not-so-choice portions of lamb leg for the preceding recipes, freeze them until you have sufficient to mince for a recipe such as this. If preferred, use good quality minced beef.

Serves 4

500 g (1 lb) finely minced lamb
½ garlic clove, crushed
1 tsp finely grated fresh ginger
1 tsp salt
1 tsp garam masala
1 tbsp ground almonds
1 tbsp besan (chick pea flour) or fine peasmeal
1 fresh green chilli, seeded and finely chopped
1 tbsp natural yoghurt

1. Trim any heavy sinews from the shank end of the leg of lamb and mince finely or grind in a food processor. If buying lamb already minced, ask the butcher for meat which has been through a fine screen.

2. Combine the remaining ingredients add the meat and mix thoroughly. Knead well until the mixture becomes very smooth and paste-like.

3. Divide the meat mix into four equal portions and shape into long sausages. Press them onto skewers that have a rectangular cross-section, as the mixture will slip on round skewers.

4. Cook over glowing coals on a barbecue grill which has been brushed with oil. Keep turning the kebabs and brush lightly with oil until brown on all sides and cooked through. Serve with rice or pitta bread and tomato and onion salad.

SOUVLAKIA

In the mood for Greek food? Try this different marinade.

Serves 6–8

1 leg of lamb, about 2 kg (4 lb), boned
125 ml (4 fl oz) dry white wine
125 ml (4 fl oz) olive oil
2 tbsp lemon juice
2 tsp dried oregano
1 garlic clove, crushed
1½ tsp salt
¼ tsp freshly ground black pepper

1. Trim off all excess fat from the lamb, leaving just a thin layer on some pieces to keep the meat succulent. Cut off the sinewy lower portion of leg and reserve it for another dish, using the choice portions only. Cut the meat into large cubes.

2. In a non-metallic bowl, combine the wine, oil, lemon juice, oregano, garlic, salt and pepper, and stir. Add the meat, cover the dish with cling film and refrigerate for a whole day or at least overnight. Turn the pieces of meat in the marinade once or twice.

3. Thread the lamb onto skewers with space between the pieces. If liked, thread pieces of dried bay leaves between the meat.

4. Cook over gently glowing coals until done, brushing frequently with the marinade. Serve with pitta bread and Greek Salad (see page 92).

See photograph on page 66·67.

SHAMI KEBAB

These minced lamb and lentil patties may be served as a main course or as appetiser-size savouries.

Serves 4 as a main dish or makes
24 hors d'oeuvres

750 g (1½ lb) finely minced lamb

1 large onion, finely chopped

4 tbsp yellow split peas or red lentils

1 tsp finely grated fresh ginger

1½ garlic cloves, crushed

1½ tsp salt

500 ml (18 fl oz) water

½ tsp garam masala

1 tbsp natural yoghurt

1 small egg, beaten

ghee (clarified butter) or oil for brushing

Filling

1 fresh green chilli, seeded and finely chopped

1 finely chopped spring onion, including green leaves

2 tbsp finely chopped fresh coriander

½ tsp finely grated fresh ginger

1. In a saucepan, combine the lamb, onion, lentils, ginger, garlic, salt and water, and bring to the boil, stirring. Cover and cook over low heat until the meat and lentils are soft, about 45 minutes, then uncover and cook, stirring occasionally, until the mixture is quite dry. Leave until cool.

2. Mix in the garam masala and yoghurt and half the beaten egg. If the mixture is not moist enough to mould, add more beaten egg. Knead well for 10 minutes or use a blender or food processor to get a smooth consistency.

3. Divide the mixture into 8 portions. Combine all the ingredients for the filling and put ½ tsp of filling in the middle of each portion, closing the meat mixture around it. Form each one into a flat patty. Cook on the barbecue hot plate, lightly greased with ghee. Serve hot with pitta bread and a salad.

—— **COOK'S TIP** ——

If making appetiser-size patties mix the filling ingredients into the meat. Cook as above and serve with Fresh Mint Chutney (see page 112) for dipping.

KOREAN BEEF SHORT RIBS

If I had to choose a favourite marinade for beef it would be the traditional Korean combination. This recipe, called *Bulgalbi*, and *Bulgogi* which is done with boneless rump or fillet, are two of the most popular in this cuisine. When you taste them you'll know why.

Serves 6 as a main dish, 8–10 as an appetiser

2 kg (4 lb) beef short ribs

125 ml (4 fl oz) soy sauce

125 ml (4 fl oz) water

6 tbsp spring onions, finely chopped

2 garlic cloves, crushed

1 tsp finely grated fresh ginger

1 tbsp sugar

½ tsp freshly ground black pepper

2 tbsp toasted, crushed sesame seeds (see Tip)

1. Ask the butcher to saw through the bones, making cubes of about 5 cm (2 inch) size. Hold the pieces on a chopping board, bone downwards, and with a sharp knife, make small cuts halfway through the meat to let the marinade penetrate. Put the meat in a saucepan, cover with cold water and bring to the boil on high heat. Boil for 5 minutes to cook off the excess fat. Drain immediately and set aside.
2. Combine the remaining ingredients in a large bowl, add the short ribs and mix well. Cover with cling film and marinate for 4 hours, turning the meat occasionally or refrigerate overnight.
3. Prepare the barbecue well ahead of time so the coals have an hour or more to achieve the steady glow necessary for successful cooking. Place the meat on an oiled grill with the bone side towards the coals, and cook until brown. Turn with tongs and cook the other side until well done. Keep turning the ribs until they are brown and crisp on all sides. Serve warm. These should be held in the fingers for eating and may be served with hot Steamed Rice or a Chinese Noodle Salad (see pages 36 and 95).

COOK'S TIP
To toast the sesame seeds, put them in a small, heavy frying pan or saucepan and shake or stir constantly over medium low heat until all the seeds are golden brown. Turn them out of the pan at once or they will continue cooking and perhaps become bitter. Cool, then pound in mortar with a pestle or grind in an electric blender or food processor.

MARINATED JAPANESE BEEF WITH SPRING ONIONS

The flavours are delicate yet appetising. No wonder Japanese restaurants are popular all over the world.

Serves 4

375 g (13 oz) Scotch fillet (rib eye steak)

3 tbsp shoyu (Japanese soy sauce)

3 tbsp mirin or dry sherry

3 tbsp sugar

1 tsp finely grated fresh ginger

16 slender spring onions

carrot slices and shredded lettuce, to garnish

1. Trim the piece of beef if necessary and half freeze it until it is firm enough to cut into very thin slices, no more than 3 mm (⅛ inch) thick.
2. Stir together the shoyu, mirin, sugar and ginger until the sugar dissolves. Pour into a flat dish and marinate the beef slices for 20 minutes.
3. Meanwhile, cut the spring onions into pieces of a size that will leave some green portion and some white extending from each end when wrapped in the beef. Wrap the beef around them.
4. Grill the rolls over a preheated oiled grill or cook on a very hot griddle plate or iron frying pan lightly filmed with oil, turning them with tongs until brown. Serve at once, garnished with the carrot and lettuce and accompanied by Steamed Rice (see page 36).

SERVING SUGGESTION
To give that decorative Japanese finish, make each slice of carrot look like a flower. Not difficult if you cut small notches around the carrot before you slice it.

See photograph on page 68.

KOREAN FIERY BEEF

Bulgogi, my other favourite Korean dish, is usually cooked at the table on a domed grill with very small openings. To cook on a barbecue, make the slices of beef large enough not to fall through the grill but so thin that cooking is a matter of seconds.

Serves 8 as a main dish, 12 as an appetiser

| 1 kg (2 lb) lean rump steak or fillet |
| marinade as for spareribs (see page 86), but in half quantities |

Bulgogi Sauce

| 4 tbsp soy sauce |
| 2 tsp sesame oil |
| 1 tsp dhwen jang or gochujang (Korean bean paste) |
| 3 tbsp water |
| 3 tbsp rice wine or dry sherry |
| 1 tsp toasted, ground sesame seeds |
| 1 spring onion, finely chopped |
| 1 tsp chilli sauce, optional |
| 1 garlic clove |
| 2 tsp sugar |

1. Cut the steak into very thin slices, partially freezing it first to make it easier to handle. Place the slices between two sheets of cling film and beat with a rolling pin until they are very flat. Cut into squares.
2. Make up the marinade in a shallow dish and marinate the beef in it for 3 hours or longer. Grill briefly over glowing coals and serve with white rice. Meanwhile, make the Bulgogi Sauce; combine the soy sauce and sesame oil in a small bowl and stir in the dhwen jang, water, rice wine, sesame seeds, spring onion and chilli sauce, if using. Crush the garlic with the sugar to make a smooth paste, then stir it into the sauce. Serve in small individual sauce bowls.

BEEF AND COCONUT FRICADELLES

An Indonesian recipe which makes a good appetiser or may be served with rice, Gado-Gado and peanut sauce as a main meal.

Serves 6

| 250 g (8 oz) fresh grated coconut |
| 500 g (1 lb) minced beef |
| 2 garlic cloves |
| 1½ tsp salt |
| ½ tsp freshly ground black pepper |
| ½ tsp dried shrimp paste, dissolved in 1 tbsp of water |
| 2 tsp ground coriander |
| 1 tsp ground cumin |
| ½ tsp ground kencur (lesser galangal) |
| 2 eggs, beaten |
| 4 tbsp coconut milk for basting |
| bamboo skewers, soaked for 1 hour |

1. In a large bowl, combine the coconut and beef. Crush the garlic with the salt to make a smooth paste and put it into a small bowl. Add the pepper, dissolved shrimp paste, the spices and the beaten eggs. Mix well, then pour the marinade over the beef and coconut.
2. Using your hands, combine the ingredients thoroughly, kneading well so that the spices are evenly distributed and the mixture is smooth. Shape the spiced meat into small balls and thread 4 onto each bamboo skewer.
3. Grill over the coals, brushing with coconut milk. If a hot flavour is desired, stir a little chilli sauce into the coconut milk. Turn and grill until browned on all sides. Serve warm or cold.

COOK'S TIP

If possible, use fresh coconut but otherwise substitute desiccated coconut and moisten it by sprinkling over 8–10 tbsp of water and rubbing gently with your fingertips until all the coconut feels moist.

See photograph on page 66·67.

HAMBURGERS GOURMANDS

There is a problem with hamburgers that every cook is already aware of. If 'hamburger mince', with its high proportion of fat, is used the fat runs, and the end result is not very nice, but if lean 'premium mince' is used the hamburgers are very dry. Here is my solution for keeping the hamburgers moist, extending the meat and giving it flavour.

Makes 6

| 500 g (1 lb) premium quality mince |
| 60 g (2½ oz) fresh wholemeal breadcrumbs |
| 4 tbsp water |
| 1 small onion, finely chopped |
| 1 stick celery, finely chopped |
| 1 or 2 cloves garlic |
| 1½ tsp salt |
| ½ tsp freshly ground black pepper |
| 1 egg, beaten |
| 1 tsp made mustard |
| 6 sesame seed buns, mayonnaise and pickles, to serve |

1. Put the meat into a large bowl. Sprinkle the breadcrumbs with the water, toss lightly to mix and add it to the meat, together with the onion and celery.
2. Crush the garlic with the salt and combine with the pepper, egg and mustard. Pour it over the meat mixture and mix thoroughly to distribute the flavours.
3. Form the mixture into 6 large or 12 medium-sized patties, handling the mixture lightly with wet hands. Place on a plate with greaseproof paper or freezer plastic between each patty. Cook on a lightly greased griddle until brown on both sides and medium rare in the centre. Serve on sesame seed buns and top with Mayonnaise (see page 108) or pickles.

--- **COOK'S TIP** ---
For a more mellow flavour, cook the onion and garlic in a spoonful of oil just until soft and golden before adding it to the mixture.

BEEF AND WHOLE-WHEAT BURGERS

This provides the perfect formula if you're trying to cut down on meat, yet love the flavours that go with good grills. The wheat used is Lebanese cracked wheat, burghul, which has already been boiled and ground to various degrees of fineness. Use a fine grade for this recipe.

Makes 12

| 1 cup cracked wheat |
| 1 tbsp dried onion flakes |
| 750 g (1½ lb) lean minced beef |
| 6 tbsp unprocessed bran |
| 6 tbsp fresh wheatgerm |
| 6 tbsp stoneground wholemeal flour |
| 2 tsp sea salt |
| ½ tsp freshly ground black pepper |
| 1 tbsp mild curry paste, optional |

1. Put the cracked wheat into a bowl and rinse a couple of times in cold water. Drain, add the dried onions and just enough cold water to cover. Leave to soak for 1 hour, then drain off excess water.
2. In a large bowl, combine the remaining ingredients and mix well. Divide into 12 equal portions and shape into patties about 10 cm (4 inches) across.
3. Barbecue on an oiled grill or griddle plate over medium heat until golden brown on both sides, and serve at once with cooked vegetables or a salad.

--- **SERVING SUGGESTION** ---
With burgers you can make meals of many international flavours, e.g. with grilled pineapple rounds they can be Hawaiian, brushed with tangy barbecue marinade they can take on Californian overtones, and with a chilli-bean sauce you have Texan Burgers.

SINGAPORE-STYLE PORK SATAY

These spicy morsels may be prepared with beef instead of pork, using a tender grilling cut.

Serves 6

750 g (1½ lb) pork shoulder
1 strip lemon rind
1 medium-sized onion, roughly chopped
2 tbsp light soy sauce
2 tbsp peanut oil
2 tsp ground coriander
1 tsp ground cumin
1 tsp ground turmeric
¼ tsp ground cinnamon
1 tsp salt
1 tsp sugar
2 tbsp roasted peanuts
purple onion and cucumber to serve
bamboo skewers, soaked for 1 hour

1. Cut the pork into small cubes, no larger than the tip of your finger. Satays are always well cooked, and the size of the meat helps achieve this.
2. Put the lemon rind, onion, soy sauce, oil, spices, salt, sugar and peanuts into a food processor or electric blender and blend to a purée. Pour the marinade over the meat, mix well and leave for at least 1 hour, longer if possible.

3. Thread 5 or 6 pieces of meat onto the bamboo skewers. The meat should be at the pointed end of the skewer only, leaving more than half the skewer free. Don't push the pieces too closely together, a little space helps them cook evenly.
4. Barbecue over moderate heat, turning so that the satays are well browned on all sides. Serve with wedges of onion and cucumber, and a bowl of Peanut Sauce (see page 110).

See photograph on page 66·67.

BARBECUED PORK CHOPS 'SURPRISE'

Imagine a succulent pork chop with a hidden treasure of a brandied apricot or spiced prune. Easy to do if you have a small, very sharp, pointed knife.

Serves 4

4 medium thick pork loin chops
4 tsp whole-grain mustard
4 tsp salad oil
¼ small garlic clove, crushed
½ tsp dried marjoram
4 brandied apricots or spiced prunes (see pages 114 and 112)

1. Trim off the skin and excess fat from the chops. With a pointed knife, make a pocket in each chop. Start on the edge where the skin and fat were trimmed, and move the point of the knife in a quarter circle making room to accommodate the fruit. Do not cut too large an opening on the outside of the chop.
2. Mix together the mustard, oil, garlic and marjoram, and rub it generously over the chops and inside the pockets as well. Put a prune or apricot inside each chop and leave at room temperature at least 30 minutes.
3. Heat the griddle plate and barbecue the chops for 6–8 minutes on each side, depending on their thickness. Finish cooking, if liked, over the coals for just a minute on each side. Serve with red cabbage cooked with apples.

SPICED JAMAICAN PORK

This is certainly spicy, but not too hot if you remember to split the chillies and remove the seeds.

Serves 6–8

750 g (1½ lb) pork neck or fillet

2 tbsp dried whole allspice

1 onion, roughly chopped

1 or 2 fresh red chillies, sliced

¼ tsp ground cinnamon

¼ tsp grated nutmeg

½ tsp freshly ground pepper

1 tsp salt

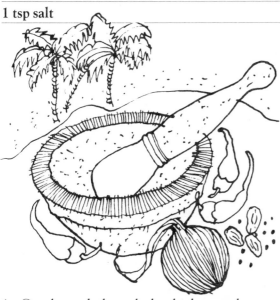

1. Cut the pork through the thickness, almost in half, so it presents a greater surface area. It will cook through more quickly. Place in a large shallow dish.
2. In mortar with a pestle, pound all the other ingredients together to form a rough spice paste, and rub it into the pork thoroughly. Cover with cling film and leave for at least 30 minutes at room temperature or, for the best results, overnight in the refrigerator for the flavours to penetrate and develop.
3. Grill over low heat for 40–45 minutes or until the pork is cooked and the outer surface is deep brown. Turn with tongs every 10 minutes. Cut the pork into thin slices on the diagonal, slanting the knife at a 45 degree angle so that the slices are larger than they would be if cut straight down. Serve with hot vegetables or salad.

ORIENTAL-STYLE PORK FILLET

A good, lean piece of pork neck or pork fillet is suitable for barbecuing because there is not a great deal of fat which will fall into the fire, causing it to flare up. You can, of course, use this same marinade on spareribs but be sure to cut off the fat first, as described in the recipe for Hawaiian Glazed Spareribs (see page 86).

Serves 6

500 g (1 lb) pork neck or fillet

1 tbsp dark soy or ketjap manis (sweet soy)

1 tbsp hoi sin sauce

1 tbsp honey

1 tbsp dry sherry

2 tsp Oriental sesame oil

2 tsp chilli sauce, optional

1 tsp finely grated fresh ginger

½ garlic clove, crushed

1. Trim any obvious fat or heavy membrane from the pork neck and cut it almost in two, to make the piece half as thick and twice as long.
2. Combine all the other ingredients in a shallow dish, add the pork and marinate for 2 hours if possible, turning it over from time to time. It may be covered with cling film and marinated overnight in the refrigerator if this is more convenient.
3. Preheat the barbecue. Thread the pork, ribbon fashion, onto skewers and place on the rotisserie, brushing with the marinade at intervals. If there is no rotisserie attachment, thread the pork onto two long skewers, one at each end of the meat. Cook, not too close to the source of heat, turning frequently and brushing with the marinade. This should take about 35 minutes in a covered barbecue. The pork should be glazed and richly coloured, well done but not overcooked. Slice finely and serve with Chinese Noodle Salad (see page 95).

See photograph on page 65.

HAWAIIAN GLAZED SPARERIBS

Tender pork spareribs are delicious, but it is almost impossible to trim all the fat off. I have found that cooking them for 20–30 minutes in a hot oven or 10 minutes in fast-boiling water before marinating, gets rid of most of the fat. When cooking there are fewer flare-ups from the fat – but always stand by with the water spray.

Serves 10–12

3 kg (6 lb) pork spareribs
3 tbsp oil
2 onions, finely chopped
2 garlic cloves, crushed
400 ml (13 fl oz) tomato purée
1 × 450 g (¾ lb) can crushed pineapple
1 tsp salt
1 tsp dry mustard
1 tsp ground ginger
4 tbsp wine vinegar
3 tbsp honey
3 tbsp light soy sauce

1. Ask the butcher to remove the skin from the pork. Preheat the oven to hot, 220C, 425F, Mark 7 and place the ribs on a rack in a roasting dish. Roast for 30 minutes, fat side upwards.
2. Meanwhile, make the sauce. Heat the oil and gently fry the onions and garlic until soft and golden. Add the tomato purée and half the liquid from the pineapple. Stir in the salt, mustard, ginger, vinegar, honey and soy sauce, and simmer until thick, stirring occasionally.
3. Remove the ribs from the oven and pour off the fat. Brush the ribs with the sauce and marinate for at least 1 hour. If a rotating spit is available, thread the spareribs onto the spit and barbecue over gentle heat for 40 minutes. Brush again with the marinade and continue cooking until the spareribs are crisp and brown. Drain the crushed pineapple well, add it to the sauce, then allow it to simmer for 5 minutes.
4. Remove the ribs from the spit, cut into 3-rib sections and serve hot with some of the sauce spooned over. Baked yams or pumpkin go well with this dish and for a green vegetable what could be more appropriate than South Sea Island Spinach (see page 33).

--- SERVING SUGGESTION ---

If you'd prefer a salad to cooked vegetables. I'd like to suggest a combination of peppery watercress and tangy orange slices.

THAI PORK AND CRABMEAT SAUSAGE

A sausage with lots of exotic flavour. It will cause a sensation, especially if you cook it the authentic Thai way, sprinkling coconut over the coals to give a delicious smoky flavour.

Serves 4

250 g (8 oz) finely minced pork
125 g (4 oz) crabmeat, cartilage removed
1 medium-sized onion, finely chopped
3 tbsp finely chopped fresh coriander
3 tbsp roasted peanuts, coarsely ground
sausage skin

Thai Curry Paste

1 hot chilli, finely chopped

1 garlic clove, crushed

rind of 1 lemon, finely grated

1 tsp dried shrimp paste or anchovy sauce

½ tsp salt

1 tbsp fish sauce

3 tbsp thick coconut milk (see page 125)

1. Put the pork, crab, onions, coriander and peanuts into a bowl.
2. To make the Thai curry paste, mix all the ingredients together in a bowl and pour this mixture over the pork and crab, kneading until it has been absorbed.
3. Slip one end of the sausage skin over the tap and run cold water through it. Then use a funnel to fill the sausage skin, not dividing into links but making one long sausage. Fasten both ends firmly with a knot. Prick the sausage in several places with a fine bamboo skewer and curl it to form a flat coil. Place the sausage in a well oiled grilling basket and barbecue at a good distance from the coals so that it takes at least 30 minutes to cook. Turn over when one side is done.
4. During the last 10 minutes, sprinkle the coconut from which the milk was extracted over the coals. The smoke will give more flavour to the sausage. If using canned coconut milk, create smoke with wood chips soaked in water.
5. When the sausage is done cut it into slices and serve with Mange Tout, Water Chestnut and Radicchio Salad (see page 94).

COOK'S TIP
This sausage mixture can also be cooked as tiny cocktail-size patties on a lightly oiled pan or griddle. Note: A ready-made Thai curry paste (called Red Curry Paste) is available from Asian stores and can also be used.

SRI LANKAN SPICED SAUSAGES

So spicy that you must have lots of rice or potatoes to eat with them. Or try a cross-culture variation, tucking a crisp, grilled sausage into crusty French bread.

Serves 6

500 g (1 lb) lean pork
250 g (8 oz) fat pork
1 tbsp coriander seeds
½ tsp ground cinnamon
½ tsp freshly ground black pepper
½ tsp freshly grated nutmeg
¼ tsp ground cloves
1½ tsp salt
3 tbsp malt vinegar
sausage skins

1. Trim any tough tissue from the meat and mince or chop it finely. Finely dice the fat and put it into a bowl with the lean pork.
2. In a dry pan, roast the coriander seeds, shaking or stirring constantly, until golden brown and fragrant. While still warm, pound in a mortar with a pestle or grind in an electric blender. Sprinkle over the pork, together with the other ground spices and the salt. Add the vinegar and mix together well.
3. Stretch one end of the sausage skin over the tap and run cold water through it, then use a funnel to force the mixture into the skin, twisting it at short intervals to make small sausages, about 12.5 cm (5 inches) in length. Don't fill the skin too tightly or the sausages may burst during cooking.
4. Prick the sausages with a fine skewer, blanch in simmering water for 5 minutes and drain. Barbecue them fairly slowly over low coals on which a few soaked chips of fruit wood are burning. Stand by with a water spray to drench flare-ups. Cook the sausages until crisp and brown.

HICKORY-SMOKED RUMP ROAST

Here's the perfect way to feed a number of people and combine the ease of a roast dinner with the incomparable flavour of meat cooked over coals and smoked with hickory chips. The marinade is complex but not overpowering. What comes through is the flavour of good beef, subtly enhanced by herbs, wine, oil and woodsmoke.

Serves 8–10

1 slice rump steak, 1.25 kg (2½ lb) and 7.5–10 cm (3–4 inches) thick
1 tbsp whole black peppercorns, coarsely crushed
1 tsp juniper berries, crushed
2 or 3 bay leaves, broken in pieces
1 tbsp finely chopped chives
1 tbsp finely chopped fresh oregano
3 tbsp dry vermouth
3 tbsp olive oil
2 garlic cloves, crushed
1 tsp salt
½ tsp ground allspice
1 tsp Worcestershire sauce

1. Ask the butcher for a slice from the small end of the rump. With a sharp knife carefully remove any pockets of internal fat, keeping the slice intact.
2. Combine the remaining ingredients in a shallow bowl and mix thoroughly. Add the beef and marinate for at least two hours, turning it over twice.
3. When the barbecue has reached the right stage for cooking, add the hickory chips which have been soaked in water.
4. Cut a small hole in the covering membrane on each side of the meat and thread it onto the spit of a rotisserie. Barbecue over low heat for 40–50 minutes, and baste frequently with the remaining marinade. If wished, cook roast potatoes in aluminium foil on the areas of the barbecue which won't interfere with the movement of the meat on the rotisserie.
5. When browned all over and firm to the

touch, transfer the meat to a serving plate and allow the beef to rest for 10 minutes before carving it into slices. Serve with the potatoes and a cooked green vegetable such as asparagus or broccoli.

COOK'S TIP

A thick slice of round steak can also be used in this recipe. I have found it every bit as good, and suggest that you also try it with the Korean marinade.

BEEF TERIYAKI

In Japanese recipes such as this one, use shoyu, Japanese soy sauce, for the correct flavour. Kikkoman, famous for its soy, also makes a mild, low salt variety.

Serves 6

1 small garlic clove
½ tsp sugar
½ tsp finely grated fresh ginger
6 tbsp shoyu sauce
6 tbsp mirin or dry sherry
6 slices of fillet steak, trimmed
2 tbsp oil

1. In a shallow bowl, crush the garlic with the sugar and mix with the ginger, shoyu sauce and mirin. Put each steak into the marinade and marinate for 30 minutes.
2. Heat a heavy griddle plate or iron frying pan and film lightly with the oil. Sear the steaks on both sides to seal, then continue cooking over lower heat until done.
3. Mix the remaining marinade with 4 tbsp of water and 2 tsp of sugar and bring to the boil. Serve with the steaks.

STEAK AU POIVRE

Crusted with crushed black pepper, steaks have marvellous flavour. No wonder this dish swept all before it in the popularity stakes . . . no pun intended!

Serves 4

2 tbsp whole black peppercorns
4 fillet steaks, 2.5 cm (1 inch) thick, trimmed
2 tbsp butter
sea salt, to taste
4 tbsp cognac

1. Crush the peppercorns coarsely in a mortar with a pestle or put them in a plastic bag and crack with a rolling pin. They must not be too finely crushed.
2. Dip both sides of the steaks in the peppercorns, pressing firmly so the meat is well coated. Let the steaks stand at room temperature for an hour.
3. Heat a barbecue griddle plate or heavy iron frying pan and when very hot, melt the butter and sear the steaks. Cook for one minute, then carefully turn them and sear the second side. Move the pan further away from the heat and continue cooking until done as you like them. Season with a grinding of sea salt.
4. Warm the cognac in a brandy warmer or small pan, ignite it and pour flaming over the steaks. Serve at once with a salad.

WHAT YOU SHOULD KNOW ABOUT BARBECUED STEAKS, CHOPS AND JOINTS

Something I've learned is that it pays to make friends with your butcher. Tell him when you're buying meat for a barbecue, and hopefully he will care enough to advise you well. One day, when I couldn't get the thick slice of rump I had hoped to cook on the rotisserie, he suggested a similar sized piece of round steak which worked very well. "I do have some rump," he said, "but it's too fresh. The round will be better for barbecuing."

Whether your preference is for a thick slice of rump, sirloin or T-bone steak, or the more economical cross-cut blade, here are some tips to give you successful results every time.

Most important of all, start the fire long before you start to cook; if there are flames it's too soon to start cooking. The fire should have reached the stage of glowing coals.

Trim all excess fat off the meat, leaving only a thin edge. With a sharp knife, make slashes through the fatty edge and the thick connective tissue between fat and lean. This prevents the meat curling during cooking. Do this with lamb or veal chops too.

The meat should be at room temperature before cooking, so take it from the refrigerator in plenty of time.

For best results, the surface of the meat should be dry, so pat with kitchen paper. Season lightly with pepper. Some cooks prefer not to salt the meat at all, but if a little salt is added *just* before cooking it does not draw out moisture. Brush the marinade on after the surface has been sealed.

Heat the grill or hotplate thoroughly before starting to cook as the high heat seals the surface of the meat, keeping the juices and flavour in. Continue cooking on lower heat until the meat has cooked to the desired stage.

Don't use a fork to turn the meat as piercing the steak lets the juices run out. Instead, have long-handled tongs handy.

Have accompaniments ready and waiting so the meat may be enjoyed as soon as it is cooked or carved.

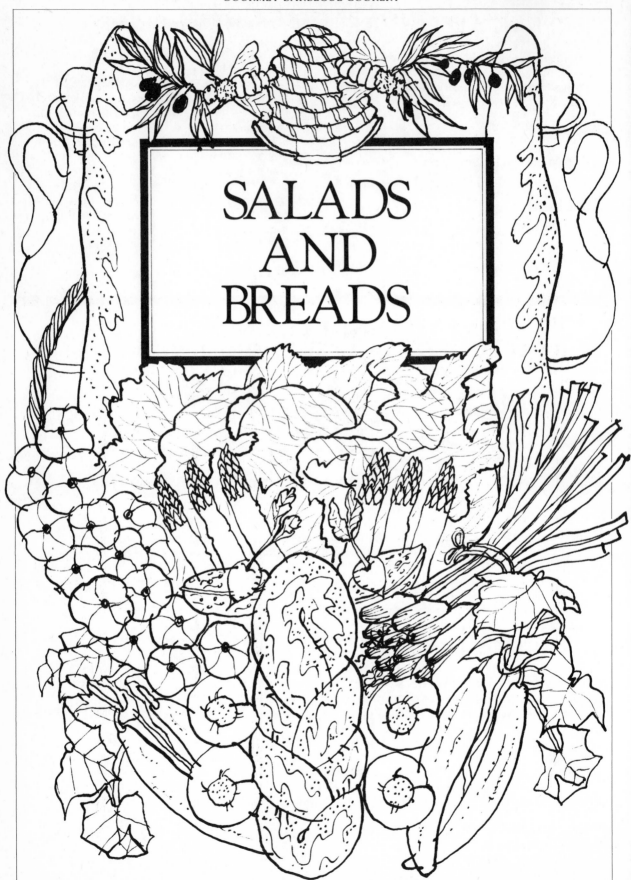

SALADS
AND
BREADS

This chapter brings you recipes that are so necessary to a good barbecue though not actually cooked over the coals themselves.

Salads, for instance. What makes such a meal complete is the crisp cool salad alongside the hot grilled food. Very important too are those crusty breads, spicy pilafs and relishes that go together with barbecued food like love and marriage.

Fresh, raw salads don't take long to make. I have also included some cooked salads (such as Pasta Salad and Lima Bean Salad (see pages 95, 97)) because they are so suitable for informal eating outdoors. If you're using dried beans which need long soaking, start preparations the day before.

Accompaniments are not merely to help fill the gaps, they carry on the theme of the meal. For instance, if you're having Souvlakia (see page 79), Greek-style lamb on skewers, it would be appropriate to serve a Greek salad with it, and a pilaf or flat bread. (Pitta bread is available from most good delicatessens.)

If you're serving Indian lamb kebabs it would be nice to make some Naan bread (see page 100) beforehand. Or, if you prefer, spicy Basmati Pilau (see page 37). With Indonesian satays, try their famous salad, Gado Gado (see page 96), lightly cooked vegetables with peanut sauce.

Salads, and other accompaniments from countries whose outstanding barbecue recipes are featured, enable you to present a barbecue meal with international flavour. These recipes have been chosen because they are suitable for advance preparation so you won't have too much to distract you while the meal is being cooked. It's only fair that the chef should also relax a little and enjoy the barbecue.

SALADE ACADEMIE

I first tasted this inspired combination of mignonette, whitloof (Belgian endive or chicory) and macadamia nuts at an Académie Culinaire Française dinner, and it has remained a firm favourite.

Serves 6–8

2 or 3 mignonette lettuce, washed and dried

3 Belgian endive chicory, washed and dried

small can pâté de foie with truffles, optional

Dressing

3 tbsp walnut oil

3 tbsp olive oil

3 tbsp white wine vinegar

salt and freshly ground black pepper to taste

3 tbsp crushed toasted macadamia nuts

1 tbsp finely chopped chives

1. Chill the greens until crisp. Chill the pâté.
2. Arrange the greens on chilled plates, the pointed leaves of endive radiating from the centre, surrounded by mignonette leaves. The pâté, if used, is to be sliced thinly and placed on a leaf of mignonette in the centre.
3. To make the dressing, whisk together the oils and vinegar and salt and pepper, until well combined. Stir in the macadamia nuts and chives, and drizzle the dressing over the greens.

SERVING SUGGESTION

Use the pâté de foie only if serving the salad as a first course – it is not necessary if the salad is an accompaniment to meat or poultry.

GREEK SALAD

There is more than one kind of salad eaten in Greece, but this is what the rest of the world thinks of as typical, with black olives and feta cheese enlivening the greens and tomatoes. In Greece this is known as *salata horiatiki* or country salad.

Serves 8

1 large Cos or iceberg lettuce, washed and drained

handful of tangy seasonal salad greens e.g. endive, escarole, washed and drained

1 green cucumber, unpeeled and finely sliced

4 firm red tomatoes, cut into 6 wedges

1 red or green capsicum (pepper), seeded and sliced

1 small onion, finely sliced

100 g (4 oz) feta cheese, diced

100 g (4 oz) Greek-style black olives

6 tbsp olive oil

3 tbsp vinegar

salt and freshly ground black pepper

1 tbsp chopped fresh oregano or 1 tsp dried

1. Tear the lettuce into pieces and put it into a large bowl. Arrange the vegetables on the lettuce, add the feta cheese and sprinkle over the black olives.
2. Whisk the olive oil, vinegar, salt, pepper and oregano together, until well combined. If liked, a crushed clove of garlic may be added. Just before serving, whisk the dressing ingredients together again (or shake in a screwtop jar), pour over the salad and toss gently.

See photograph on page 45.

RUSSIAN SALAD

Diced cooked vegetables make a salad that does not wilt. However, it is best kept in the refrigerator until required.

Serves 6

2 boiled potatoes, peeled and diced

2 boiled carrots, peeled and diced

2 cooked or canned beetroot, peeled and diced

125 g (4 oz) cooked green peas

1 small onion, finely chopped

1 pickled cucumber, sliced

250 ml (½ pint) mayonnaise (see page 108)

salt and freshly ground black pepper, to taste

6 tbsp soured cream

2 tbsp chopped parsley

1. Combine the potatoes, carrots and beetroot in a bowl with the peas, onion, cucumber and mayonnaise. Season to taste and mix well.
2. Press lightly into a bowl, cover with cling film and chill until required. Turn out on serving plate, spoon the soured cream over and sprinkle with the chopped parsley. Alternatively, serve in the bowl.

WATERCRESS SALAD WITH CHERRY TOMATOES

Peppery watercress is good to serve with rich meats. If preferred, use it with other salad greens.

Serves 6

1 bunch watercress

1 punnet cherry tomatoes, washed

Herbed Oil and Vinegar Dressing (see page 106)

1. Wash the watercress well in at least two changes of water. Discard any tough stems and yellowed leaves and break the cress into sprigs. Combine the watercress and tomatoes in a bowl, cover and chill. At serving time, toss with the dressing.

AVOCADO AND STRAWBERRY SALAD

Well, what a happy accident that all I had on hand for a salad was lettuce, avocados and strawberries. It turned out so special that it has become a favourite. Avocados for a salad should be ripe but still reasonably firm.

Serves 8

1 Cos lettuce
1 large iceberg lettuce, washed and dried
1 punnet strawberries, washed, hulled and cut in half
2 firm ripe avocados
Strawberry Vinegar and Cream Dressing (see page 107)

1. Close to serving time, arrange the lettuce in a bowl, peel and slice the avocados and place on the lettuce. Top with the strawberries. Just before serving, pour the dressing over and toss gently.

See photograph on page 48.

ARMENIAN PILAF WITH FRUITS

Excellent with just about any of the meat or poultry recipes, but particularly good with lamb.

Serves 6

500 g (1 lb) long grain rice
3 tbsp ghee (clarified butter)
1 large onion, finely chopped
1 stick cinnamon
750 ml (1¼ pts) chicken stock or water
250 ml (8 fl oz) fresh orange juice
grated rind of 1 orange
4 tbsp sultanas
4 tbsp chopped, dried apricots
2 tbsp currants
2 tsp salt

1. If the rice needs washing, wash it well in cold water and let it drain in a colander for at least 30 minutes.
2. Heat the ghee in a large, heavy saucepan and fry the onion and cinnamon stick over medium heat until the onion is soft and golden. Add the rice and fry, stirring, for about 5 minutes or until the grains are coated with butter.
2. Add the stock, orange juice and grated orange rind, the dried fruit and salt. Bring to a fast boil, then turn the heat down very low, cover the saucepan with a well fitting lid and cook for 20 minutes. Remove from the heat and leave uncovered for 5 minutes to allow the steam to escape, then fluff the rice with a fork. Serve warm or cool.

— COOK'S TIP —

Rice keeps its heat in the pan for about an hour, but if serving it cool, turn it out of the saucepan onto a dish while it is still warm, or it will be inclined to mould itself to the pan instead of being fluffy.

AVOCADO, ORANGE AND SPANISH ONION SALAD

The colours, flavours and textures make this a salad to remember.

Serves 6–8

3 large seedless oranges
2 firm, ripe avocados, halved and peeled
1 lettuce, Cos or iceberg, washed and drained
2 mild purple onions, sliced and pushed into rings
3 tbsp raspberry or red wine vinegar
6 tbsp salad oil
½ tsp sea salt
freshly ground black pepper, to taste

1. With a sharp knife, peel the oranges to remove the white pith and expose the flesh. Cut them into thin slices. Remove the avocado seed, lay the cut side down on a board and cut across into crescent-shaped slices.
2. Line a salad bowl with the lettuce and arrange the oranges, onion rings and avocado slices on the lettuce, cover with cling film and refrigerate. Whisk together the remaining ingredients for a dressing, and just before serving pour it over the salad and toss gently.

VEGETABLE SALAD WITH FRESH COCONUT

Don't attempt this salad with dried coconut. My hints and tips on using fresh coconut are on page 125.

Serves 6–8

250 g (8 oz) tender green beans
2 medium-sized carrots, cut into julienne strips
1 red capsicum (pepper), cut into julienne strips
250 g (8 oz) fresh bean sprouts, washed and drained thoroughly
half a fresh coconut, grated
1 medium-sized onion, finely chopped
1 tsp salt
juice of 1 lemon

1. String the beans and cut into 5 cm (2 inch) lengths. If the beans are broad, slice them down the centre so they look like julienne strips. Blanch the beans, carrots and capsicum separately in lightly salted boiling water until half tender, drain and plunge into ice water. Drain thoroughly.
2. Remove any loose skins and straggly tails from the bean sprouts. Toss all the vegetables together in a bowl.
3. Combine the coconut, onion, salt and lemon juice, sprinkle it over the vegetables and toss to mix. Cover and keep chilled until required.

MANGE TOUT, WATER CHESTNUTS AND RADICCHIO

Mange tout or snow peas are lovely to eat raw when young and tender. If those you buy are past the first flush of youth, blanch them in boiling water for 1 minute and refresh under cold water.

Serves 6

125 g (4 oz) mange tout (snow peas) or sugar snap peas

1 × 230 g (8 oz) can water chestnuts

1 radicchio, washed and crisped

Oriental Dressing (see page 107)

1. String the mange tout and blanch if necessary. Slice the water chestnuts into two or three discs each. Tear the radicchio into bite-sized pieces and use to line a salad bowl.
2. Scatter the mange tout and water chestnuts over the radicchio, and shortly before serving toss with the dressing.

COOK'S TIP
If radicchio is not in season, use mignonette lettuce or escarole.

See photograph on page 28.

PASTA SALAD

Colourful and with a tangy tomato-flavoured mayonnaise, this salad not only tastes good, it also looks great on the plate. I created it for my children, and though they're quite grown up now, it's still popular.

Serves 4

1 tbsp oil

250 g (8 oz) tortiglioni (twists)

1 quantity blender mayonnaise (see page 108)

2 tbsp tomato paste

½ garlic clove, crushed

2 tbsp finely chopped parsley

125 g (4 oz) cooked green peas, optional

1. Bring a large amount of lightly salted water to the boil, add the oil to prevent it boiling over then pour in the pasta. Cook until just tender, but still firm to the bite, *al dente*, then run some cold water into the pan to stop cooking. Drain in a colander, shaking it well to get rid of all the water.
2. Combine the mayonnaise, tomato paste and garlic, and mix well, then pour it over the pasta and toss gently until the pasta is coated. Transfer to serving bowl and garnish with the parsley and peas, if using. Serve warm or cold.

CHINESE NOODLE SALAD

Ideal for a picnic and particularly good to serve with any barbecued fish or meat which has an Oriental flavour, for instance Grilled Trout with Spring Onions and Ginger, Barbecued Spareribs, or Chicken and Mushroom Sausage.

Serves 4–6

225 g (8 oz) ribbon-style egg noodles

6 spring onions, finely sliced

6 tbsp chopped fresh coriander leaves

225 g (8 oz) fresh bean sprouts, rinsed and brown tails removed if necessary

Dressing

4 tbsp soy sauce

4 tbsp peanut oil

2 tbsp sesame oil

2 tbsp lime or lemon juice

1. Drop the noodles into a pan of fast-boiling salted water until tender but not mushy. Test a piece after 4 minutes, it should be slightly firm to the bite. Run cold water into the pan and drain well in a colander, rinsing with cold water to make sure the noodles don't overcook.
2. Cut the noodles into short lengths and combine with the spring onions, chopped coriander and bean sprouts.
3. Combine all the ingredients for the dressing and whisk or shake them together well. Pour it over the noodles and toss well. Chill until needed.

See photograph on page 65.

GADO GADO

This is an Indonesian salad of vegetables which are cooked briefly and are still crisp. Quantities are flexible, according to how many are being served.

Serves 8

250 g (8 oz) fresh bean sprouts, washed and picked over

250 g (8 oz) tender green beans, stringed

half a small cabbage, sliced and central stem removed

2 large carrots, cut into strips

3 large potatoes, boiled, then peeled and sliced

250 g (8 oz) pressed bean curd

oil for frying

4 hard boiled eggs

1 green cucumber, sliced

half quantity Peanut Sauce (see page 110)

1. Pour boiling water over the bean sprouts, then refresh in cold water. Cut the beans, into bite-size lengths and cook briefly in boiling water until just tender. Boil the cabbage in salted water until half tender. Blanch the carrots so they are tender but still crisp. Drain all the vegetables well and arrange on a long serving platter.

2. Deep fry the pressed bean curd until golden brown all over, drain on absorbent kitchen paper and cut into slices. Place in the centre of the vegetables. Slice the hard boiled egg and cucumber and arrange it around the dish.
3. Gently heat the peanut sauce with enough coconut milk or water to give a thick pouring consistency, and spoon it over the salad before serving.

See the photographs on page 66·67.

TABBOULEH

For this healthy parsley and cracked wheat salad known in Lebanon as *Tabbouleh*, a fine grade of cracked wheat is used. This is called burghul and is available at Greek and Middle Eastern delicatessens. Since the wheat has been boiled and dried, it needs no cooking.

Serves 6

125 g (4 oz) fine burghul

1 small bunch fresh mint, chopped

1 large bunch parsley, chopped

1 bunch spring onions, finely sliced

125 ml (4 fl oz) olive oil

150 ml (5 fl oz) lemon juice

1½ tsp salt

freshly ground black pepper, to taste

3 firm, ripe tomatoes, diced

Cos lettuce

1. Wash the burghul 3 or 4 times in cold water, cover with cold water and soak for 10 minutes, then squeeze out the water and place in a sieve to drain.
2. Combine the mint, parsley, onions and wheat. Whisk together the oil, lemon juice, salt and pepper and pour over, rubbing lightly between the fingers to distribute flavours.
3. Add the diced tomatoes shortly before serving, toss lightly to mix. Line a bowl with Cos lettuce, pile the tabbouleh in the middle, and serve with extra Cos lettuce leaves for scooping up the salad.

CRUNCHY PINEAPPLE SALAD

This salad gives an old favourite new interest by adding the sweetness of pineapple and the crunchiness of toasted almond slivers.

Serves 8–10

half a small white cabbage

3 carrots, scrubbed and grated

2 green peppers, cut into julienne strips

1 × 450 g can (1 lb) crushed pineapple, drained

125 ml (4 fl oz) Oil and Vinegar Dressing (see page 106)

250 ml (8 fl oz) mayonnaise (see page 108)

1 tbsp sugar

50 g (2 oz) slivered almonds, toasted

1. Choose a tightly packed cabbage, shred finely and soak in iced water for 1 hour. Drain well. Combine all the vegetables and pineapple in a bowl.
2. Whisk together the Oil and Vinegar Dressing, mayonnaise and sugar. Pour it over the vegetables and mix thoroughly. Transfer to a serving bowl and sprinkle with the toasted almonds.

LIMA BEAN SALAD

This is a substantial cooked salad which requires time for the beans to soak.

Serves 8–10

500 g (1 lb) dried lima beans

2 tsp salt

2 tsp turmeric

1 quantity mayonnaise (see page 108)

paprika, to garnish, optional

1. Put the dried beans into a saucepan with water to cover them by at least 3 cm (1¼ inches). Bring to the boil, turn off the heat, cover and allow the beans to soak for 2 hours. Drain and add fresh hot water, the salt and turmeric, then simmer for 1 hour or until tender. Drain.
2. Toss the beans with the mayonnaise, spoon them into a serving dish and sprinkle, if liked, with a little paprika.

CARROT, PECAN AND RAISIN SALAD

With the sweetness of carrots and dried fruit, the crunch of toasted pecans, this is an ideal salad to accompany barbecued food.

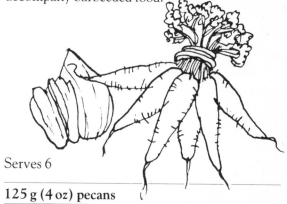

Serves 6

125 g (4 oz) pecans

60 g (2 oz) seedless raisins or sultanas

3 medium-sized carrots, coarsely grated

¼ white cabbage, shredded

lemon juice to taste, or a creamy salad dressing

1. Toast the pecans in a moderate oven 180C, 350F, Mark 4 for 8–10 minutes; cool and break into pieces. Add the pecans and raisins to the carrots and cabbage, squeeze lemon juice over and toss well to mix.

GERMAN DILLED POTATO AND CUCUMBER SALAD

It was in the famous Hofbraühaus in Munich that I came across this unusual potato salad, served with Vienna sausage. Good with any kind of sausage, I'd say.

Serves 4

1 green cucumber
500 g (1 lb) floury potatoes
3 tbsp white vinegar
3 tbsp salad oil
salt and white pepper to taste
2 tbsp snipped fresh dill

1. Peel the cucumber, leaving a vestige of green. Slice it finely, sprinkle with a little salt and set aside while the potatoes cook.
2. Boil the potatoes until tender, drain, then peel and mash while still hot. Add the vinegar and oil, and season to taste.
3. Pour off the liquid from the cucumber and mix the cucumber slices into the mashed potato, together with the fresh dill.

CUCUMBERS WITH SOURED CREAM

For weight watchers the soured cream may be replaced with yoghurt.

Serves 6

2 large green cucumbers, peeled and thinly sliced
2 tsp salt
½ garlic clove, crushed
½ tsp finely grated fresh ginger
300 ml (11 oz) soured cream
lemon juice, to taste

1. Put the cucumbers into a bowl, sprinkle with the salt and leave for 1 hour. Pour off the liquid and rinse briefly to remove any extra salt.
2. Mix the garlic and ginger into the soured cream, stir in cucumbers and mix thoroughly. Taste and add the lemon juice and a little more salt if necessary. Cover and refrigerate until serving time.

See photograph on page 117.

BEETROOT AND YOGHURT COOLER

This makes a piquant and brightly coloured relish to serve with kebabs and rice.

Serves 8

1 bunch beets, cooked and peeled or 1 × 800 g can spiced beetroot
400 ml (14 fl oz) natural yoghurt
salt and spiced vinegar, to taste

1. Dice the peeled beetroot or, if using canned beetroot, drain reserving 3–4 tbsp of the liquid, and chop roughly. Mix the diced beets and yoghurt, adding salt and spiced vinegar to taste. If using canned beets, stir the reserved liquid into the yoghurt, before adding the beets.

CRACKER BREAD

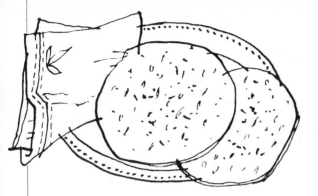

This is a variation on Armenian flat bread, *Lavosh*, paper thin, delightfully crisp, and flavoured with sesame and poppy seeds. Very easy to make if you have a pasta roller.

Makes 12 crisp breads, 25 cm × 15 cm (10 × 6 inches)

300 g (11 oz) plain flour
1 tsp sugar
½ tsp salt
1 large egg
150 ml (¼ pt) water
2 tbsp melted butter

To Glaze and Decorate

1 egg beaten with 2 tbsp water
3 tbsp sesame seed
2 tbsp poppy seed
1 tsp caraway seed, optional
coarse salt

1. Sift the flour, sugar and salt into a bowl. Make a well in the centre and pour in the egg, water and butter. Mix with your finger tips and form the dough into a ball. Knead lightly until it forms a smooth, elastic dough.
2. Alternatively, make the dough in a food processor. Put the flour, sugar and salt into a food processor fitted with a steel blade. Beat the egg and mix it with the water and butter. Start the motor and slowly pour the liquid through the feed tube. Process for only as long as it takes the ingredients to form a ball.
3. Wrap the dough in cling film and chill for 1 hour.
4. Divide the dough into 12 equal portions and, on a well floured surface, roll each one into a thin oval shape. (Or pass between the rollers of a pasta machine until very thin.) Place on baking sheets, brush with beaten egg and water, then sprinkle lavishly with the combined seeds and sparingly with the coarse salt. Cook in an oven preheated to Mark 5.
5. Bake the lavosh until pale golden and very crisp. Cool on a wire rack and store in an airtight container. Serve with unsalted butter, or by itself.

─────── COOK'S TIP ───────

I have found that a large plastic bag in a warm cupboard above the stove is the perfect place to keep lavosh crisp for a week or more.

FATTOUSH

This is a Middle Eastern salad which includes toasted pitta bread added just before serving.

Serves 6–8

1 large green cucumber
3 firm ripe tomatoes, diced
1 red capsicum (pepper), seeded and thickly sliced
1 green capsicum (pepper), seeded and thickly sliced
small bunch parsley, washed and roughly chopped
6 spring onions, cut into short lengths
1 garlic clove, crushed
1 tsp salt
4 tbsp olive oil
6 tbsp lemon juice
1 or 2 rounds pitta bread

1. If the skin and seeds of the cucumber are tender, simply wash and slice it. Otherwise peel, halve, scoop out the seeds and then slice it thickly. Put all the vegetables into a large bowl.
2. Combine the garlic, salt, oil and lemon juice and whisk together well. Toss the vegetables in the dressing.
3. Grill the pitta bread, watching it carefully, until very crisp, then break it roughly into bite-sized pieces. Mix into the salad at the last moment, then serve.

NAAN

Although not as well known as chapatis, these yeast-risen loaves, rich with butter and egg, are the aristocrats of Indian bread.

Makes 8 loaves

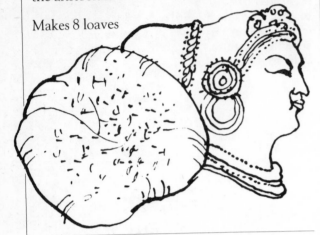

25 g (1 oz) fresh yeast or 2 tsp dried yeast

185 ml (6½ oz) warm water

1 tbsp sugar

125 ml (4 fl oz) natural yoghurt

1 egg, beaten

125 ml (4 fl oz) ghee (clarified butter) or butter

2 tsp salt

500 g (1 lb) plain white flour

3 tbsp extra yoghurt

2 tbsp sesame seeds or black cumin seeds

1. Sprinkle the yeast over 50 ml (2 fl oz) warm water and stir until it has dissolved. Add 1 tsp sugar, stir and leave in a warm place for 10 minutes or until it starts to froth. (If it doesn't froth, the yeast is too old – get a fresh batch.)
2. Stir the yoghurt until smooth, then mix it with the rest of the sugar, remaining 125 ml (4 fl oz) warm water, egg, ghee and salt. Stir in the yeast mixture.
3. Measure half the flour into a bowl, make a well in the centre and pour in the liquid, beating well with a wooden spoon until it is smooth.
4. Add the remaining flour a little at a time and when it is too stiff to beat with the spoon, knead by hand until a stiff dough has formed. Knead hard for 10 minutes or until the dough becomes smooth and elastic, using as little extra flour as possible.

 Form the dough into a ball and let it rest while washing the bowl in hot water. Dry the bowl well and grease it, adding the dough and turning it over so both sides are greased. Cover and leave

in a warm place for 20–30 minutes or until doubled in bulk and a finger pushed into the dough leaves an impression. Punch down dough, divide into 8 balls and leave for 10 minutes.
5. Bake in a oven preheated to very hot, 230C, 450F, Mark 8. Put two ungreased baking trays into the oven to preheat.
6. On a smooth, lightly floured surface, pat the dough into circles. Keep them thin in the centre with a little rim around the edge. Pull one end outwards, making a teardrop shape. They should be a handspan long and about half as wide at the base. Brush with some of the extra yoghurt and sprinkle with sesame or black cumin seeds.
7. Place 2 or 3 loaves on each baking tray and bake for 10 minutes or until golden and risen. Serve warm or cool with tandoori style chicken, lamb kebabs or other Indian dishes.

─── COOK'S TIP ───

The owner of the Omar Khayyam restaurant in Singapore gave me the secret of his Khayyam Naan. He mixes some crushed garlic into the yoghurt with which the naan is brushed, and on it he sprinkles flaked almonds.

HERB BUTTER RING LOAF

Here's bread that doesn't need to be cut – it can be pulled apart easily, because small pieces of dough are dipped in butter and placed in the baking tin.

Serves 6

700 g (1½ lb) plain white flour
3 tsp salt
15 g (½ oz) fresh yeast or 2 tsp dried yeast
450 ml (¾ pt) warm water
1 tsp sugar
6 tbsp chopped chives or other fresh herbs
125 g (4 oz) butter, melted

1. Sift the flour and salt into a large warm bowl. Dissolve the yeast in 100 ml (4 fl oz) of the warm water, and stir in the sugar. Add the yeast mixture to the remaining mixture.

2. Make a well in the centre of the flour, pour in the yeast liquid and mix to a stiff dough. Knead vigorously on a floured surface for 10 minutes or until the dough is no longer sticky but smooth and elastic. Form into a ball and let it rest while washing and greasing the bowl.

3. Place the dough in the bowl, turn it over so the top is greased, and cover the bowl with a tea towel or cling film. Leave in a warm place until the dough has risen to twice its volume. Punch down and knead lightly to eliminate any air bubbles. Form into balls about the size of a walnut, or pat the dough out flat and cut it into finger-size strips.

4. Have ready two ring tins or loaf tins, lightly greased. Mix the chopped fresh herbs into the melted butter and dip each piece of dough in the mixture before dropping it into the tins. Cover and leave to rise once more.

5. Bake the bread in an oven preheated to 200C, 400F, Mark 6 for 10 minutes, then reduce the heat to moderate, 180C, 350F, Mark 4 and continue baking for 25–30 minutes or until the loaves are golden brown on top. To test if they are done, remove from the tin and rap with your knuckles on the bottom; it should sound hollow. Cool on a wire rack, then wrap in aluminium foil and store or freeze if preparing ahead.

QUICK GOURMET BREAD

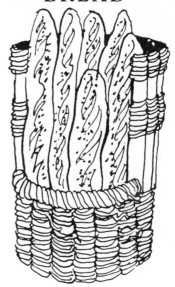

No time to bake bread? Never mind, so much can be done with bought crusty loaves.

Use French bâtons or Italian-type long loaves. Cut into thick slices almost to the bottom crust and spread both sides of each slice with one of the flavoured butters or spreads such as Orange and Hazelnut Spread or Mustard Butter (see pages 106, 105).

Wrap the loaf in aluminium foil with the join on top. Place on the barbecue until heated through or bake in a hot oven.

In addition, make up your own combinations. Herb and Garlic Butter is popular and needs 1 small garlic clove crushed with ½ tsp salt, and 2 tbsp finely chopped parsley, chives, dill or other herbs combined with 125 g (4 oz) softened butter.

— **COOK'S TIP** —

If you're short of warm, draught-free spots in which to rise the dough, do what I sometimes do and put the bowl in the dishwasher which has just finished a wash and is all warm and steamy! Or run hot water into the sink, place the bowl on an upturned dish so it is above water level, and cover the sink with a cloth to keep the warmth in. When the weather is sunny, just pop the bowl into a plastic bag and leave in a sunny spot.

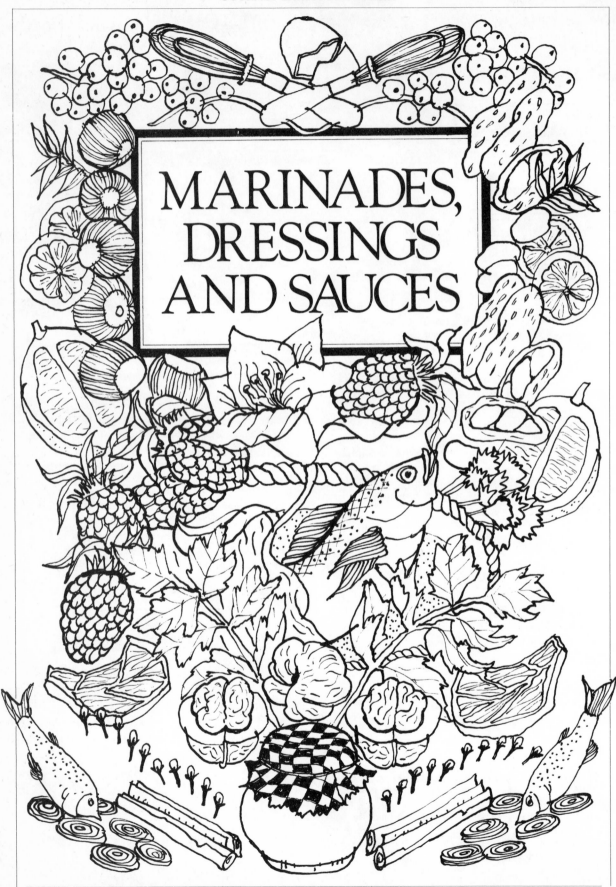

MARINADES, DRESSINGS AND SAUCES

Let's be realistic – a marinade can only do what you let it. The more time it has to work its magic, the more it will transform even the humblest ingredient. A little planning ahead so that your meat or poultry sits in the marinade overnight and the rewards will be great.

Even the best of prime beef, the tenderest lamb or poultry, the freshest fish, are all improved when married with a fragrant marinade. If you have no time to marinate, try a dry marinade with concentrated flavour, rubbing the spices and herbs into the meat, poultry or fish, instead of adding them to oil or wine.

Another option is to serve a plain grill with a sauce which has reduced until the flavours are intensified. One of the most memorable meals I have enjoyed was simply barbecued rabbit fillets. But oh, the sauce that accompanied them! This was at one of England's foremost restaurants, three stars in the Michelin guide and no one could deny that skill and training went into creating the dish.

The point I am making is that even with the simplest meal there should be something that makes it outstanding. In a barbecue meal, your marinades, dressings and sauces are what add that flavour fillip.

A tip I would like to pass on is to make a little more of the marinade than you will need for marinating, set some aside and serve it as a sauce. You'll find that even if some of the flavours get cooked out in the barbecuing process, they are confirmed and intensified when the reserved mixture is poured over after cooking. Not too much, just enough to underscore the original theme.

Something I've noticed is that certain cookbooks require the reader to make vast amounts of marinade – both unnecessary and wasteful. I have tested all the recipes and the amounts given are ample to flavour the given quantity of food. There is no need for the main ingredient to swim in it! However, if you plan to increase quantities, i.e. six chickens instead of one, please multiply the marinade recipe accordingly.

To lift a barbecue meal out of the camp fire class and into the gourmet category I depend on fragrant fruit vinegars, oils such as walnut and hazelnut, the zest of citrus fruits, fresh and dried herbs and of course, those mainstays of the imaginative cook, exotic spices. Some of these are easily found, but you may have to search around for others.

Hazelnut oil is not cheap, but so beautifully redolent of this favourite nut that it may be combined with two or three parts of maize or sunflower oil (or other tasteless oil) and still impart its flavour. Good quality cardamom or saffron is pricey and not usually found in the corner shop, but worth searching for and worth the outlay. Buy small amounts, use them while they are fresh, and they will more than repay you in flavour dividends.

The vinegars, too, are well worth buying. Such a small amount is needed and a bottle should last for months. Just wait until you taste the Strawberry Vinegar and Cream Dressing (see page 107) – tart, fragrant, redolent of strawberries on a summer afternoon – and you too will agree that it is a worthwhile addition to the pantry shelf.

HAZELNUT OIL AND RASPBERRY VINEGAR MARINADE

This is really superb, lovely with lamb but just as good with veal, chicken, even seafood.

Makes about 60 ml (2 fl oz)

| 2 tbsp hazelnut oil |
| 2 tbsp raspberry vinegar |
| ½ tsp salt |
| 2 tsp honey |
| 1 tbsp chopped fresh dill |
| generous grinding of black pepper |

1. Put all the ingredients into a shallow bowl and whisk with a fork until thoroughly mixed and the honey has dissolved. It is sufficient for ½ kg (1 lb) of lamb chops, poultry or fish fillets.

WALNUT OIL AND WHITE WINE MARINADE

I first tried this marinade on tuna steaks, and found it delicious. If you like the flavours, use the marinade for chicken or other meats.

Makes about 100 ml (3½ fl oz)

| 2 tbsp walnut oil |
| 2 tbsp sunflower or maize oil |
| 4 tbsp Chardonnay or other white wine |
| 1 small garlic clove, crushed with salt |
| freshly ground black pepper |
| ½ tsp made mustard |
| 1 tbsp chopped fresh dill |

1. Combine all the ingredients in a bowl and whisk together. It is sufficient to marinate ½ kg (1 lb) of meat, poultry or fish.

ORANGE AND HAZELNUT OIL MARINADE

On white fish, which is delicate in flavour, I like to use marinades which don't disguise the natural taste. The combination of orange and hazelnut is so good that I also used it in a brush-on spread for crusty bread, which I served with the barbecued fish.

Makes about 90 ml (3 fl oz)

| ½ tsp finely grated orange rind |
| 2 tbsp orange juice |
| 1 tbsp hazelnut oil |
| ¼ tsp salt |
| ¼ tsp white pepper |

1. Whisk all the ingredients together with a fork in a shallow dish and marinate the fish for about 30 minutes. It is sufficient for 4 medium-sized fish fillets.

CITRUS AND CINNAMON MARINADE

A delicate and fragrant marinade that echoes the flavours of the Spanish drink, Sangria. Try it on lamb, chicken or fish. Just for fun, serve Sangria as the accompanying beverage and see if your guests recognise the flavours in a different setting.

Enough for 6 chops or fillets

| finely grated zest of 1 large orange and 1 large lemon |
| 125 ml (4 fl oz) red wine (with fish, use white wine) |
| 1 stick cinnamon, broken in pieces |
| ½ tsp salt |
| freshly ground black pepper, to taste |

1. Combine all the ingredients in a large shallow dish, add the meat, chicken or fish,

turning the pieces until well coated. Leave overnight or for at least 2 hours at room temperature. Grill over medium heat – not too close to glowing coals – until done. Serve with a salad.

KASHMIRI-STYLE MARINADE

I adapted this from a traditional recipe for lamb, and discovered that this marinade also gives great flavour to fish. Use a thick-fleshed, firm fish and marinate it for 20–30 minutes only.

The marinade is sufficient for 500 g (1 lb) boned and cubed lamb, or a boned and rolled shoulder or loin which is to be cooked in one piece.

4 tbsp natural yoghurt

1 tsp grated ginger

1 small garlic clove, crushed with ½ tsp salt

2 tsp lemon juice, optional

1 tsp ground cumin

1 tsp honey

¼ tsp each of freshly ground black pepper, cardamom and turmeric

¼ tsp chilli powder (optional)

⅛ tsp each of ground cloves and cinnamon

1 tbsp oil

1. Put the yoghurt into a bowl and mix in all the spices and seasonings. Pour it over the meat and mix well. Cover and marinate overnight if possible, otherwise for about 1 hour in a tightly covered container. Thread the meat onto skewers and cook until crisp and brown on the outside.

2. If using fish, cook it in an oiled, wire basket over glowing coals, turning it once during cooking so that both sides are browned but not overcooked. To test if the fish is ready, flake it with a knife at the thickest part. It should be opaque when done.

3. Serve with Spiced Rice or Naan (see pages 37, 100) and a salad of tomatoes and spring onions.

MUSTARD BUTTER WITH GREEN PEPPERCORNS

It is possible to buy whole grain mustard already combined with green peppercorns, but if you can't find any, simply add 2 tsp of green peppercorns, drained from their brine and lightly crushed, to 2 tbsp of Pommery-style mustard.

Makes about 90 ml (3 fl oz)

4 tbsp melted butter

2 tbsp green peppercorn mustard

2 tsp finely chopped parsley

1 tsp dried tarragon, crumbled

1. Combine all the ingredients in a bowl and set aside half for serving with the fish after it has been barbecued. Spread the mixture over the fillets and marinate for several hours. Serve the barbecued fish with the reserved mustard butter.

—— COOK'S TIP ——
This mixture is also very good on bread which is to be heated in aluminium foil. It makes a nice change from garlic butter and is used in the same way – applied to both sides of thick slices which are cut almost to the bottom crust.

HERB BUTTER FOR LAMB

When my daughter served this it was such a hit that we realised it had to be included in this book. The lamb was a boned, rolled loin roasted in the oven, but as we've found out, it goes equally well with barbecued or grilled chops.

Makes about 150 ml (5 fl oz)

---

100 g (4 oz) butter, at room temperature

1 tbsp honey

½ tsp finely grated fresh ginger

½ garlic clove, crushed

¼ tsp salt

¼ tsp freshly ground black pepper

2 tsp fresh rosemary

2 tsp grated tangerine rind

1 tbsp tangerine juice

---

1. Soften the butter, then work it in with the honey, ginger, garlic, salt and pepper, rosemary, tangerine rind and juice.
2. Stir until smooth, then spoon it into a small bowl and keep cool. Serve small pats on warm lamb, and it will melt into a most delicious butter sauce.

ORANGE AND HAZELNUT SPREAD

When using orange rind remember to grate only the coloured portion. This is where the fragrance is; if you go through to the white pith it will impart a bitter taste.

Makes about 150 ml (5 fl oz)

---

1 French or Vienna loaf, or other suitable crusty bread

finely grated rind of 1 large orange

3 tbsp hazelnut oil

6 tbsp corn or sunflower oil

½ tsp sea salt

½ tsp white pepper

2 tbsp finely chopped parsley

---

1. Slice the bread thickly, almost to the bottom crust. Combine the remaining ingredients in a bowl, mixing thoroughly. Brush the spread on both sides of each slice. Wrap the bread in aluminium foil and place over the barbecue to heat through. Serve with barbecued fish which has been cooked in the matching marinade.

OIL AND VINEGAR DRESSING

Invaluable to have on hand. Not only does it dress salads, but it becomes a base for a marinade to which you add the flavours you feel the main ingredient calls for . . . fresh herbs such as thyme, oregano, tarragon, parsley, dill; crushed green or pink peppercorns; ground spices; a dash of liqueur; the fragrant zest of citrus, or the appetising aroma of garlic.

Makes about 300 ml (10 fl oz)

---

4 tbsp wine vinegar

1 tsp salt

½ tsp freshly ground black pepper

½ tsp dry mustard

250 ml (8 fl oz) olive oil or salad oil

---

1. Put the wine vinegar, salt, pepper and mustard into a bowl and whisk or beat with a fork.
2. Gradually add the oil, beating until the dressing is well combined and smooth. Always beat again just before serving. If you find it easier, combine the ingredients in a screwtop jar and shake the bottle well before serving.

GARLIC DRESSING

Please yourself whether you want the full effect of garlic or simply a stimulating whiff. In the former instance, crush 1 small garlic clove with the salt specified in the dressing and whisk in with the oil and vinegar. For just a gentle hint, lightly bruise the garlic clove, toss it in with the oil and remove before serving.

HERB DRESSING

Make one quantity of Oil and Vinegar Dressing with or without the garlic and add 2 or 3 tbsp finely chopped fresh herbs such as parsley, chives, thyme, dill, oregano or marjoram.

ORIENTAL DRESSING

The flavours are distinctive. Dress a salad to go with one of the Chinese, Japanese or Korean barbecue dishes.

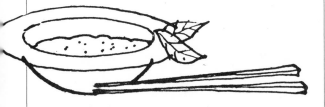

Makes about 350 ml (11 fl oz)

½ tsp finely grated fresh ginger
½ garlic clove, crushed
1 tsp salt
1 tbsp light soy sauce
2 tbsp Chinese wine or dry sherry
4 tbsp sweet Chinese vinegar or other mild vinegar
125 ml (4 fl oz) peanut oil
2 tbsp Oriental sesame oil

1. Combine all the ingredients except the oils in a bowl and whisk well. Slowly pour in the oils, whisking constantly until thoroughly mixed. Store in a refrigerator and shake or whisk just before using.

STRAWBERRY VINEGAR AND CREAM DRESSING

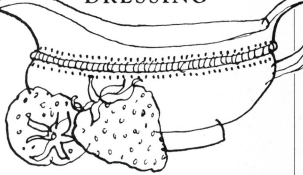

Originally I invented this for a particular salad, one with avocado slices, strawberries and lettuce. Then I discovered that it goes well with any salad of mixed greens, imparting a subtle strawberry flavour to the dressing.

Makes about 165 ml (5½ fl oz)

3 tbsp strawberry vinegar
3 tbsp walnut or hazelnut oil
3 tbsp maize or sunflower oil
3 tbsp mayonnaise (see page 108) (not salad cream)
3 tbsp double or thick cream
¼ garlic clove, crushed
½ tsp sea salt
¼ tsp white pepper
2 tsp sugar

1. Put all the ingredients into a bowl and whisk together until evenly combined and smooth. Store in a screwtop glass jar in the refrigerator until needed, and give it a good shake before pouring over the salad.

GREEN GODDESS DRESSING

Another useful dressing to have ready in the refrigerator. Serve with salads, or as a sauce for cooked vegetables. Imagine what it does for a potato salad! And that's not all – try it on barbecued fish or shellfish.

Makes about 400 ml (13 fl oz)

250 ml (8 fl oz) thick mayonnaise (see below)
½ garlic clove, crushed
2 tsp finely chopped canned anchovy fillets
3 tbsp finely chopped spring onion leaves
3 tbsp finely chopped parsley
1 tbsp tarragon vinegar
125 ml (4 fl oz) thick soured cream
freshly ground sea salt and black pepper

1. Combine all the ingredients thoroughly in a bowl, check for seasoning and add salt and pepper to taste.

CLASSIC MAYONNAISE

If you don't think your beating arm can last the distance, use a hand-held electric beater or mixer. The secret of successful mayonnaise is to have the ingredients at room temperature, and to add the oil *very* slowly at first. Olive oil is best, but if you find it too strong mix it with a light tasteless oil such as sunflower. Use the proportions you prefer.

Makes about 300 ml (½ pt)

2 egg yolks
2 tbsp vinegar
½ tsp sea salt
¼ tsp white pepper
250 ml (8 fl oz) oil
2 tbsp lemon juice
1 tbsp boiling water

1. Put the egg yolks into a warm bowl and remove the challazah or transparent string that is attached to each yolk. Whisk the yolks to blend, then add the vinegar, salt and pepper.

2. Pour in the oil very gradually, a few drops at a time while whisking the mixture constantly. When about half the oil is in, it can be added in a thin stream until all the oil has been incorporated. Stir in lemon juice, then the boiling water. Store in a jar in the refrigerator.

WHOLE EGG BLENDER MAYONNAISE

This is very quick to make in an electric blender. Remember that mixtures with egg in them must be stored in the refrigerator, and this applies to mayonnaise (above) and salads made with mayonnaise. To prevent the mayonnaise curdling, all ingredients must be at room temperature.

Makes about 250 ml (8 fl oz)

1 egg
2 tbsp white vinegar
½ tsp salt
½ tsp white pepper
1 tsp dry mustard
1 tsp sugar
250 ml (8 fl oz) olive or salad oil

1. Put all the ingredients except the oil into an electric blender. Blend for 10 seconds on low speed. Through the hole in the cap of the blender, start pouring in the oil very gradually, a few drops at a time. As the mixture thickens, the oil may be added in a thin stream. When all the oil has been incorporated, switch off the blender, transfer the mayonnaise to a jar and store in the refrigerator.

AIOLI SAUCE

This is nothing more than mayonnaise with garlic. To the basic blender mayonnaise recipe, add 3 or 4 garlic cloves crushed with the measured salt in the recipe. This may be added at the beginning, or stirred in at the end.

MAYONNAISE WITH GREEN PEPPERCORNS

This is a super sauce to serve with just about everything. Use home made mayonnaise or a good bottled one, but remember it must be thick mayonnaise and not salad dressing.

Makes about 250 ml (8 fl oz)

250 ml (8 fl oz) mayonnaise (see page 108)
1 tbsp crushed green peppercorns in brine
2 tbsp finely chopped fresh dill
1 tbsp finely chopped pickled gherkin
1 tsp horseradish cream

1. Stir all the flavourings into the mayonnaise; store in a covered jar in the refrigerator.

SAUCE REMOULADE

Once again, a good mayonnaise is the base for this sauce which lends zest to meat, poultry and seafood.

Makes about 300 ml (½ pt)

250 ml (8 fl oz) mayonnaise (see page 108)
1 tbsp finely chopped pickled gherkin
2 tsp chopped capers
1 tbsp French mustard
1 tsp finely chopped parsley
½ tsp each chopped tarragon and chervil
½ tsp anchovy paste

1. Stir all the flavourings into the mayonnaise and store it in a refrigerator until required.

SPICY APRICOT MARINADE AND SAUCE

This is a good example of how a marinade doubles as a sauce, cutting down on preparation time. Good with chicken pieces, duck (with the fat removed) or smaller birds halved and flattened.

Makes 400 ml (13 fl oz)

50 g (2 oz) dried apricots
125 ml (4 fl oz) dry red wine
125 ml (4 fl oz) water
3 whole cloves
1 dried red chilli, seeds removed or 1 tsp dry mustard
2 garlic cloves, crushed
1 tbsp brown sugar
1 tsp salt

For Sauce

125 ml (4 fl oz) wine
1 tbsp brown sugar

1. Put the apricots, wine, water, cloves, chilli and garlic into a stainless steel saucepan and bring slowly to the boil. Simmer for 2 minutes, then turn the heat off and leave covered for 1 hour or until the apricots are soft.
2. Put the contents of the saucepan into an electric blender or food processor and add the brown sugar and salt. Blend to a smooth purée.
3. Pour half the purée into a dish for marinating. If using chicken pieces, slash the flesh to enable the marinade to penetrate. Cover and leave for about 2 hours.
4. Return the remaining marinade to the saucepan, wash out the blender jug with the extra wine and add it to the pan with the sugar. Bring to the boil and simmer, uncovered, for a minute or two. Turn into a bowl and serve as a sauce.

INDONESIAN PEANUT SAUCE

A most popular sauce in Indonesia, Malaysia and Singapore, it is usually served with Satays and Gado Gado. But you don't have to reserve it for dishes that are Asian in character. The basic mixture, before the addition of liquid, is an absolutely great spread on crackers.

Makes about 400 g (13 oz) sauce base

8 tbsp peanut oil
1 tsp dried garlic
3 tbsp dried onion flakes
2 large dried chillies
1 tsp dried shrimp paste or anchovy paste
2 tbsp lemon juice
2 tbsp soy sauce
1 × 357 g (12 oz) jar crunchy peanut butter
2 tbsp raw sugar
coconut milk or water for mixing

1. Heat the oil in a small frying pan, not letting it become too hot because the dried garlic and onion burn easily. Put the garlic in a fine wire mesh strainer and lower it into the oil for a few seconds until golden. Lift out immediately and turn onto absorbent kitchen paper. Do the same with the onion flakes, not letting them become too dark. Drain and cool.
2. In the same oil, fry the whole chillies until they are puffed and crisp, about 1 minute. Drain and cool. Discard the stalks and seeds, and chop the chillies into small pieces.

3. Fry the shrimp paste next, crushing it with the back of a spoon. Add the lemon juice and soy sauce, then remove from the heat and stir in the peanut butter. Leave the mixture until cold before mixing in the chopped chillies, onion and garlic flakes and the sugar. Stored in a screw-topped glass jar in the refrigerator, it will keep for months.
4. To serve, gently heat the required amount with enough coconut milk or water to give a thick pouring consistency.

See photograph on page 66·67.

SWEET CHILLI SAUCE

For those who like the pungency of chillies, this is irresistible with just about any meal but particularly good on barbecued meats, especially sausages and chops. It is guaranteed to add zing even when you haven't had time for marinating. Makes a large amount of sauce which keeps well.

Makes about 1 litre (1½ pt)

250 g (8 oz) fresh red chillies
750 g (1½ lb) sugar
750 ml (1¼ pt) white vinegar
350 g (12 oz) sultanas
3 garlic cloves, crushed
1 tbsp salt
1 tbsp finely grated fresh ginger

1. Be sure you wear rubber gloves when handling the chillies. Discard the stems and split the chillies lengthways. Scrape out and discard the seeds unless you want an extra hot sauce. Chop the chillies roughly and grind them in an electric blender with enough vinegar to facilitate blending.
2. Put all the ingredients into a large enamel or stainless steel saucepan and bring to the boil. Simmer gently until the sultanas are very soft. Cool, then purée in a blender or food processor or rub through a sieve. Pour into sterilised bottles and seal.

COOK'S TIP
Try adding just a teaspoon of this sauce to mayonnaise or other creamy dressings.

GUACAMOLE

This popular Mexican-style avocado sauce may be served as a dip for corn chips, crackers or crudités.

Serves 8

2 large, ripe avocados
½ onion, finely chopped
1 firm, ripe tomato, seeded and finely diced
2 serrano or jalapeno chillies, finely chopped
2 tbsp finely chopped fresh coriander
1 tbsp lemon juice or to taste
salt and freshly ground black pepper, to taste

1. Make the guacamole shortly before serving, to lessen the chances of the mixture discolouring. Halve the avocados lengthways, remove the seeds and reserve. Peel the avocados or scoop out the flesh with a spoon, then mash it with a fork.
2. Stir in the remaining ingredients, season to taste and pile it into a serving bowl. Place one of the avocado seeds in the centre until serving time as it helps prevent darkening. Cover tightly with cling film and refrigerate until serving time.

TKEMALI SAUCE

A sauce to serve with Shashlyk or Oriental barbecued duckling. Choose small, sour prunes for the best flavour.

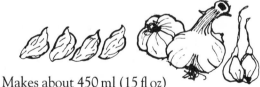

Makes about 450 ml (15 fl oz)

250 g (8 oz) dried prunes
2 garlic cloves, crushed
4 tbsp chopped fresh coriander
salt and freshly ground black pepper to taste
2 tbsp lemon juice, or to taste

1. Put the prunes into a small saucepan with enough water to cover and bring slowly to the boil. Turn off the heat, cover the pan and leave for 30 minutes or longer until the prunes are soft. Remove the seeds and put the prunes into a food processor or electric blender with the garlic and coriander.
2. Blend to a purée, adding sufficient prune liquid to facilitate blending, while not making the purée too thin. Return the liquid to the saucepan and bring to the boil, add salt and pepper to taste. Pour into a bowl and stir in the lemon juice. Serve at room temperature.

BARBECUE SAUCE AMERICANA

This is a popular sauce based on tomato ketchup with added flavourings. Use on steaks, chops, spareribs, chicken or hamburgers. Brush sparingly over the meat towards the end of cooking only as this sauce burns easily. Serve the rest separately as a spoon-on sauce.

Makes about 300 ml (10 fl oz)

185 ml (6½ fl oz) tomato ketchup
1 tbsp Worcestershire sauce
1 tbsp vinegar
1 tbsp brown sugar
1 tsp dry mustard
1 tsp Mexican-type chilli powder
dash Tabasco sauce
3 tbsp oil
1 garlic clove, crushed

1. Combine all the ingredients in a shallow bowl, except the oil and garlic.
2. Heat the oil in a small heavy saucepan and gently cook the garlic until golden. Add the marinade and simmer gently for a couple of minutes. Cool and store in a jar until required.

CUCUMBER AND SESAME RELISH

This is a tart and garlic flavoured Burmese salad which goes well with most dishes as long as those who partake are fond of garlic.

Serves 4

1 large green cucumber
500 ml (1 pt) water
125 ml (¼ pt) malt vinegar
1 tsp salt
6 tbsp peanut oil
1 tbsp Oriental sesame oil
1 tsp dried garlic flakes
2 tbsp dried onion flakes
2 tbsp sesame seeds

1. Peel the cucumber thinly, halve lengthways and remove the seeds with a spoon. Cut the cucumber into 5 cm (2 inch) lengths and then into strips the thickness of a finger.
2. In a stainless steel or enamel saucepan, bring the water, vinegar and salt to the boil, drop in the cucumber strips and boil until they look transparent – but don't let them soften too much. Drain immediately and cool.
3. Heat the oils on low heat and fry the garlic until pale golden; remove immediately with a wire spoon. Fry the onions until brown and remove quickly as it is only too easy to burn dried onion and garlic. Drain both on absorbent paper. Reserve the oil in the pan.
4. In a dry pan, toast the sesame seeds, shaking the pan or stirring constantly, until they are golden brown. Immediately turn out onto a plate to cool. When the reserved oil has cooled, sprinkle 2 tbsp over the cucumbers, add the onion, garlic and sesame seeds and toss lightly. Serve cold.

FRESH MINT CHUTNEY

Fresh herb chutneys as prepared in Indian homes have no resemblance to what the western world calls chutney, in spite of Major Grey's reputation. Serve as a dip with Seekh Kebabs or other Indian dishes.

Makes about 200 ml (7 fl oz)

125 g (4 oz) fresh mint sprigs
2 spring onions, chopped
1 fresh green chilli, seeded and chopped
2 tsp sugar
1 tsp salt
6 tbsp lemon juice

1. Wash the mint and put half the leaves into an electric blender or food processor with the remaining ingredients.
2. Blend to a purée, then with the blender running, gradually add the rest of the mint. It may be necessary to add a little more liquid, lemon juice or water, to facilitate blending. Pack into a small bowl, cover with cling film and refrigerate until required.

SPICED PRUNES

Put a jar of these on the table, they make a wonderful relish with any meal. They also make welcome gifts, and look good in a fancy glass jar with a ribbon tied around the top.

500 g (1 lb) dessert prunes
250 g (8 oz) sugar
250 ml (8 fl oz) white wine vinegar
250 ml (8 fl oz) water
1 quill cinnamon
6 whole cloves
1 tsp whole mustard seeds
1 tsp allspice (whole pimento seeds)
1 bay leaf
½ tsp salt

1. Pack the prunes into a clean glass jar.
2. In a stainless steel or enamel saucepan bring the sugar, vinegar, water and all the spices to the boil, simmer for 3 minutes, then cool slightly before pouring it over the prunes. Cover tightly and leave for at least a week or until the prunes swell and soften.

COOK'S TIP
If using smaller, harder prunes than the soft dessert variety, soak them in water overnight, then simmer until soft. Drain and use the liquid in the vinegar and spice mixture.

DESSERTS
AND DRINKS

When you're set to cook outdoors and all fired up, as it were, you may want to do everything from appetisers to desserts over the coals.

If you're experienced at handling barbecue fires you may be able to manage, but chances are everything will flow more smoothly if some starters are produced in the kitchen. The dessert too could be prepared beforehand and carried to the picnic place.

However, at the end of a barbecue there's generally a fair amount of heat still emanating from the coals and if you have fruit already foil-wrapped and ready to cook, more than likely everyone will think they've never tasted anything as good.

A barbecue with a griddle plate lets you have more choice with desserts – thick, fluffy griddlecakes with buttered syrup are a natural.

You can ring the changes and serve them with sugared berries or fruit purée. For something really special, serve a scoop of vanilla ice cream with hot syrup and a sprinkling of crushed Vienna almonds or praline. The syrup can be heated in a stout pan over the coals and the crushed almonds carried in an airtight plastic container. If you're too far from home to have access to your freezer, pack the ice cream on dry ice in an insulated container.

STRAWBERRIES GRAND MARNIER 'EN BARQUETTE'

If you cook strawberries for too long they go pale and lack-lustre. But wrap them in aluminium foil and give them just a few minutes on the heat, and they make a fine finish to a meal.

Serves 6

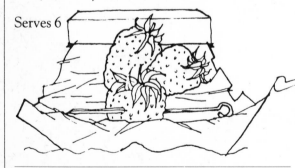

| 1 punnet firm ripe strawberries |
| 4 tbsp caster sugar |
| 4 tbsp Grand Marnier or Cointreau |
| whipped cream, to serve, optional |
| bamboo skewers, soaked for 1 hour |

1. Wash the strawberries, hull them quickly and dip them into caster sugar whilst wet, so the sugar clings.
2. Thread the strawberries onto bamboo skewers and place on a double thickness of aluminium foil. Pour the liqueur over each skewer, making sure the sides of the foil are turned up so the liqueur cannot escape. Seal the foil with a fold on top.
3. Place the boats on the barbecue grill for 3 or 4 minutes. Serve the strawberries wrapped up, so guests can slide them (and the delicious juices in the packet) onto a dessert plate for eating as soon as they are cool enough. Pass a bowl of whipped cream if wished.

BRANDIED APRICOTS

Sheer extravagance, to tuck one of these into a pork chop or steak . . . but nice. Also delicious served on vanilla ice cream.

| 500 g (1 lb) best quality dried apricot halves |
| brandy |
| 375 g (13 oz) sugar |
| 250 ml (8 fl oz) water |

1. Put the apricot halves into a wide glass jar with a tight stopper, or into a plastic container with a snap-on lid. Pour over enough brandy to cover the apricots, replace the stopper tightly and leave for at least a week.

2. Put the sugar and water into a saucepan and stir over low heat to dissolve the sugar. Boil the syrup for 5 minutes. Cool slightly. Drain the brandy from the apricots, and mix it with the syrup. Fill the container of apricots to the brim with brandied syrup and replace the lid tightly. Keep for as long as possible before using.

PEARS WITH PRUNES AND PORT

Large, firm pears are best for this, and it is easier to core and fill those with a round shape rather than long narrow ones.

Serves 4

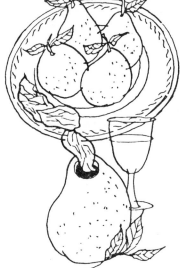

4 large, soft dessert prunes
4 tbsp port
4 firm William or other round pears
4 tsp sugar

1. Soak the prunes in the port overnight. Wash the pears but don't peel them or remove the stem. Use an apple corer to remove the core, working from underneath the pear.
2. Push one prune into the hollow of each pear then place it onto a double square of aluminium foil. Sprinkle over the remaining port and 1 tsp of sugar. Bring the foil up over the stem and twist it together to form a package.
3. Barbecue over moderate heat for 10–15 minutes depending on the size and firmness of the pears. Serve warm. If liked, a spoonful of extra port may be poured over.

See photograph on page 118·119.

STUFFED APPLES WITH RAISINS AUX RHUM

This is the by-product of another recipe testing. The rum-soaked raisins were intended for adding to ice-cream and they happened to be there while I was preparing desserts for the barbecue. This recipe yields more rum raisins than you need for six apples, but I'm sure you'll think of many other uses for them, such as serving them between fluffy griddlecakes with whipped cream.

Serves 6

250 g (8 oz) brown sugar
250 ml (8 fl oz) water
half a vanilla pod
125 ml (4 fl oz) dark rum
500 g (1 lb) sun-dried seedless raisins
6 large cooking apples
6 tsp butter
6 tbsp brown sugar

1. Put the sugar and water in a heavy saucepan with the vanilla pod and cook over medium heat, stirring until the sugar has dissolved, then simmer for 5 minutes. Remove from the heat and stir in the rum and raisins. Leave to cool, then transfer it to a glass jar and set aside for at least a week.
2. Peel and core the apples, then put each one on a square of double thickness aluminium foil. Fill the centre of each apple with the rum-soaked raisins and top each one with 1 tsp of butter, then sprinkle over 1 tbsp of brown sugar.
3. Enclose in the foil and barbecue over medium hot coals for 12–15 minutes or until the apples are soft but still hold their shape. Serve warm, with cream if wished.

—— COOK'S TIP ——
For children, fill the apples with raisins which have not been soaked in rum, and add a little orange juice or syrup to moisten, before topping with butter and brown sugar.

CARIBBEAN BARBECUED BANANAS

Bananas are absolutely ideal for barbecue cooking, they even come already wrapped!

Serves 4

| 4 large, ripe bananas |
| 2 tbsp melted butter |
| 4 tsp caster sugar |
| 4 tbsp dark rum |
| whipped cream, to serve |

1. With the point of a small sharp knife, slit the skin of each banana lengthways so when the skin is peeled back, the top half of the banana is exposed. Place the bananas, skin-side down, on the grill and barbecue until the skins are black and the fruit is slightly soft.
2. Brush the exposed part of the bananas with melted butter and, with a long-handled teaspoon, sprinkle over the caster sugar. When the sugar has melted, transfer the bananas to individual plates and remove the skin.
3. Heat the rum in a small pan, pour a little over each fruit and ignite with a match. When the flames die, having exhausted the alcohol and leaving only flavour, serve with the whipped cream as an accompaniment.

BRANDIED CREAM PEACHES

Be sure you buy freestone peaches for this or any other recipe that requires them to be halved and stoned.

Serves 4

| 4 medium peaches |
| 50 g (2 oz) butter, melted |
| 4 tbsp caster sugar or soft brown sugar |
| 4 tbsp brandy, optional |
| single cream, to serve |

1. Halve the peaches with a stainless steel knife and dip them in the melted butter. Put two halves onto a double thickness square of aluminium foil, sprinkle with the sugar and pour over 1 tbsp of brandy, if using.
2. Bring the foil up and fold together to form a parcel so the juices cannot escape. Place on the barbecue grill for about 10 minutes or until the peaches are soft but not mushy.
3. Serve in the parcels, or open the foil and slide the peaches onto a plate. Pass with a jug of cream.

See photograph on page 120.

PINEAPPLE SPEARS WITH KIRSCH

Use only ripe, sweet pineapple for this dessert.

Serves 8

| 1 small, ripe pineapple |
| caster sugar, to taste |
| 8 tbsp kirsch |
| ice cream or cream, to serve, optional |

1. With a sharp, stainless steel knife, cut off the crown of leaves and a slice from the bottom of the pineapple. Stand it upright and cut off a thin layer of skin.
2. To remove the 'eyes', placed neatly in rows, make a series of diagonal cuts on either side of the rows, removing three at a time. This saves waste and gives the fruit a decorative finish.
3. Cut the pineapple in half lengthways, then in quarters and finally in eighths. Cut out and discard the hard woody core in the centre. Place each spear of pineapple on a double strip of aluminium foil, sprinkle with sugar to taste and 1 tbsp of kirsch. Fold the foil so the juices cannot escape and place on the barbecue to heat through. Serve warm with ice cream or cream if wished.

See photograph on page 118·119.

Rajasthani-style Quail (page 72) with Cucumbers with soured cream (page 98) and Arroz verde (page 37).

OVERLEAF
Apricot and strawberry kebabs (page 121); Glazed fruit kebabs (page 121); Pineapple spears with kirsch (recipe above) and Pears with prunes and port (page 115).

ORANGES IN CARAMEL

This is so easy, it's almost cheating. Isn't it amazing how you discover short cuts when you're in a hurry! This method of getting the butter and sugar between the orange slices is quicker than most.

Serves 4

4 large seedless oranges

50 g (2 oz) firm, cold butter

4 tbsp soft brown sugar

1. Peel the oranges with a small sharp knife, removing all the skin and white pith. Cut each orange into 4 thick slices and re-assemble each one on a square of double aluminium foil.
2. Cut the butter into 16 small, flat slices. Roll them in the sugar so they are thickly covered, and put a little butter between each slice of orange and one on top. Sprinkle the remaining sugar over and wrap the oranges in the foil.
3. Place on the edge of the barbecue for 10 minutes or long enough to melt the butter and sugar, and serve hot with cream for those who want it. A spoon and fork are useful for breaking the orange slices and taking up the caramel syrup.

See the photograph opposite.

APRICOT AND STRAWBERRY KEBABS

Since these fruit are in season at the same time, use this colourful combination on the barbecue.

Serves 6

1 punnet of firm ripe strawberries

9 firm ripe apricots

100 g (4 oz) caster sugar

6 tbsp apricot brandy, optional

whipped cream, to serve, optional

1. Wash and hull the strawberries. Wash and

Brandied cream peaches (page 116) and Oranges in caramel (recipe above).

halve the apricots. Roll the damp fruit in caster sugar to coat.
2. Thread the fruit onto skewers allowing three apricot halves to each skewer, and placing strawberries within each hollow and on either end.
3. Place the fruit on double strips of aluminium foil, and bring the foil edges up to form a boat, then pour 1 tbsp of apricot brandy into each. Fold the foil over to enclose and place them on the barbecue for 6–8 minutes. Lift carefully from the grill so the juices don't run out, and put a parcel on each plate. Pass the whipped cream.

See photograph on page 118·119.

GLAZED FRUIT KEBABS

A combination of fruit grilled on a skewer until glazed makes a simple and refreshing dessert.

Serves 4

2 oranges

2 bananas

1 apple

1 pear

juice of 1 lemon

6 tbsp caster sugar

8 cubes of bread

25 g (1 oz) melted butter

1. With a sharp knife, peel the oranges, removing all the zest and white pith. Cut each orange into quarters, then across into eighths. Peel the bananas and cut into chunks the same size as the orange pieces.
2. Peel the apple and pear, and cut them into quarters lengthways, then across into eighths. Squeeze the lemon juice over to prevent discolouration. Toss all the fruit together in a bowl with 4 tbsp caster sugar.
3. Brush the cubes of bread with melted butter on all surfaces, and roll in the remaining caster sugar.
4. Thread the bread and fruit onto flat metal skewers, beginning and ending with a piece of bread. Grill over medium hot coals until lightly browned. Serve warm.

See photograph on page 118·119.

ORANGE YEAST BUNS

These buns may be prepared weeks ahead and frozen. The nice thing about them is that, wrapped in aluminium foil and reheated, they taste as if they've been freshly baked.

Makes 24 rolls

200 ml (7 fl oz) milk
125 g (4 oz) sugar
2 tsp salt
125 g (4 oz) butter
25 g (1 oz) fresh yeast or 2 tsp dried yeast
125 ml (4 fl oz) warm water
1 egg, beaten
500 g (1 lb) plain flour

Filling

250 g (8 oz) caster sugar
2 tbsp finely grated orange rind
100 g (4 oz) sultanas
50 g (2 oz) butter, melted

1. Scald the milk until it starts to rise in the pan, remove from the heat and then stir in the sugar, salt and butter. Stir until the sugar has dissolved and the butter has melted. Cool until lukewarm.
2. Sprinkle the yeast over the warm water in a large, warm bowl and stir until dissolved. Add the milk mixture, beaten egg and half the flour. Beat with a spoon or electric mixer until smooth.
3. Beat in the remaining flour to form a stiff batter. If necessary add 100 g (4 oz) of flour to make the right consistency.
4. Put the dough into a greased bowl, cover with cling film or aluminium foil and refrigerate for at least 2 hours, or as long as 4 days. If required immediately, allow the dough to rise in a warm place until doubled in bulk, then punch it down, pushing your fist into the centre.
5. Knead the dough lightly to eliminate any air

bubbles and divide it in two equal portions. On a floured board, roll out one portion to a large rectangle of 45.5 × 23 cm (18 × 9 inches). Brush with half the melted butter.
6. To make the filling, combine the sugar, orange rind and sultanas. Sprinkle half over the dough and roll it up like a Swiss roll, starting at the longest side. Cut the roll into 12 slices with a sharp knife and place them in a well buttered sandwich cake tin, 23 cm (9 inch) in diameter. Repeat with the remaining dough and filling.
7. Cover the rolls with a clean cloth and leave in a warm, draught-free place to rise for about 1 hour or until doubled in volume. Preheat the oven to moderately hot, 190C, 375F, Mark 5 and bake for 15 minutes, then reduce the heat to 170C, 340F, Mark 4 and bake for a further 15–20 minutes or until risen and golden.
8. Remove the orange rolls from the pans while hot, allow to cool, them wrap tightly in foil. Reheat on the barbecue when needed. Unwrap the foil and pull the rolls apart.

COOK'S TIP

If making ahead and freezing, thaw completely before placing on the barbecue. If the barbecue has a cover which acts like an oven, it won't matter if the rolls are frozen, but they will require at least 25 minutes to reheat.

GRIDDLECAKE STACKS WITH BUTTERED SYRUP

Watch the young people come running when they see what you're barbecuing! Have the syrup heated and ready, and be prepared to work at top speed to meet the demand. This can either be served with the Buttered Syrup below or with Grand Marnier Sauce as a variation.

Serves 6

250 g (8 oz) self raising flour
1 tsp baking powder
¼ tsp salt
75 g (3 oz) butter
350 ml (12 fl oz) milk
1 tsp vanilla essence
2 tbsp caster sugar
3 eggs, separated
ghee (clarified butter), for greasing

Buttered Syrup

75 g (3 oz) unsalted butter

250 ml (8 fl oz) maple syrup or golden syrup

1. In a bowl, sift the flour, baking powder and salt together.
2. In a small pan, melt the butter, remove from the heat and pour in the milk, then add the vanilla essence and sugar.
3. Beat the yolks in a bowl, stir in the milk and butter mixture, add the dry ingredients all at once and whisk well until the batter is smooth. The batter may be made up to this point, covered with cling film and refrigerated until required.
4. To make the Buttered Syrup, melt the butter in a small heavy saucepan, then add the syrup and heat through without boiling.
5. Shortly before cooking, whip the egg whites in a clean bowl until they are stiff, then gently fold them into the batter. Drop the batter by spoonfuls onto a preheated griddle plate, lightly greased with ghee. Cook until bubbles form on top, then with a flat spatula, turn the griddlecakes over and cook the other side. Serve in stacks of 3 with warm syrup poured over.

COOK'S TIP

If more convenient, use a small ladle to measure the batter and make larger griddle cakes – in which case one or two per serving is more appropriate.

SAUCE GRAND MARNIER

For more sophisticated tastes, serve the griddlecakes with a sauce reminiscent of that on *Crêpes Suzette*.

Serves 6

50 g (2 oz) unsalted butter

50 g (2 oz) sugar

250 ml (8 fl oz) orange juice

1 tsp finely grated orange rind

6 tbsp Grand Marnier

1. Melt the butter in a small, heavy pan, add the sugar and cook until it turns golden. Add the orange juice and orange rind and stir over medium heat until the sugar has dissolved.
2. Remove from heat and stir in half the Grand Marnier. Place the griddlecakes in small stacks, then pour the syrup over and around them. Heat the remaining Grand Marnier, ignite and pour it over the griddlecakes. Serve hot.

CREAMY HOT CHOCOLATE

I first tasted this wickedly rich beverage at the famous Rumpelmayers on Central Park South, New York, and experimented until I came up with a formula which is very very similar. Use the best chocolate you can afford.

Serves 4

150 g (5 oz) dark eating chocolate

250 ml (8 fl oz) single cream

500 ml (16 fl oz) milk

2 tsp Dutch cocoa

2 tsp sugar

1 tsp cornflour

½ tsp vanilla essence or pinch cinnamon

white marshmallows, to toast

1. Chop the chocolate and melt it over hot water or in a microwave oven, taking care no moisture gets into it.
2. Heat the cream and all but 4 tbsp milk in a saucepan, stirring, until almost boiling. Stir half the liquid into the melted chocolate and mix well until smooth, then return the chocolate mixture to the saucepan and set over low heat.
3. Mix the cold reserved milk with the cocoa, sugar and cornflour to make a smooth paste. Stir it into the chocolate mixture in the saucepan and whisk until it comes to the boil and thickens slightly. Add the vanilla and whisk briskly until foamy. Pour into tall, narrow cups and float a toasted marshmallow on top.

COOK'S TIP

Fondue forks or long, two-pronged cooking forks are ideal for toasting marshmallows.

SANGRIA

The flavours are similar to Honeyed Mulled Wine, but this is a much lighter drink, more suited to warm weather.

Serves 10

250 g (8 oz) sugar

250 ml (8 fl oz) water

1 quill cinnamon

1 large lemon

2 oranges

2 bottles red wine

soda or sparkling mineral water

crushed ice

1. Put the sugar, water and cinnamon into a saucepan and cook, stirring until the sugar has dissolved. Simmer for 5 minutes, then cool.
2. Slice the lemon and oranges, put them into a large bowl and pour the syrup over. Cover and refrigerate for a few hours.
3. Mix the syrup and fruit with the wine, add plenty of crushed ice and stir well. Add soda water to taste. Serve very cold.

HONEYED MULLED WINE

When the weather is cold this hot, spicy red wine is a welcoming drink.

Serves 12

2 bottles claret or burgundy

6 tbsp honey

2 quills cinnamon

5 cardamom pods, bruised

4 whole cloves

2 strips orange or lemon rind, optional

1. Put all the ingredients into a heavy enamel or stainless steel saucepan and place over very low heat, allowing the spices to infuse the wine with flavour. Stir to dissolve the honey.
2. Just before it reaches simmering point turn off the heat, cover the pan and leave until required. Ladle into cups and serve hot.

SPICED TEA PUNCH

Very refreshing and just the thing for those who prefer not to drink alcohol.

Serves 8

3 tbsp good quality tea leaves

1 lt (1¾ pt) boiling water

1 quill cinnamon

3 whole cloves

3 whole cardamom pods

250 g (8 oz) sugar

375 ml (12 fl oz) cold water

125 ml (4 fl oz) lemon juice

500 ml (1 pt) orange juice

crushed ice or ice cubes

chilled soda or mineral water

lemon or orange slices, to decorate

1. Put the tea in a pot and pour over the boiling water. Leave for 5 minutes, then strain it into a large bowl.
2. Put the spices into a saucepan with the sugar and cold water, bring to the boil and simmer for 5 minutes. Cool, then strain into the bowl. Add the fruit juices and just before serving, lighten the punch with soda water. Pour the punch over crushed ice into tall glasses and decorate each glass with a slice of lemon.

COCONUT MILK

Coconut milk is one of the most misunderstood and misrepresented of foods. To begin with, the clear liquid inside a coconut is *not* coconut milk, it is coconut water or juice, good for drinking when the nut is young and fresh. Writers so often refer to this as coconut milk that it is going to take years to rectify the misunderstanding. Having grown up in a tropical country where coconuts are used daily, with our own trees in the garden to supply our needs, I know whereof I speak!

Coconut milk is the milky liquid extracted from the grated flesh of mature fresh coconuts or reconstituted from desiccated coconut (dried shredded coconut). Good quality coconut milk in cans is also becoming more available. Another method is to dissolve a portion of the solid block known as creamed coconut which is readily available in many countries.

But there is nothing quite as delicious as fresh coconut milk so here is how to go about it.

Coconut milk is extracted in two stages, the first yielding "thick coconut milk" and the second, "thin coconut milk". Use a mixture of both extracts when a recipe calls for coconut milk unless thick milk or thin milk is specified. Coconut milk is perishable, and what is not used immediately should be frozen.

Using fresh coconut: The first thing to know is how to choose a good coconut. When buying a coconut, shake it to make sure it is full of water. You should hear the juice inside. The shell should be dry, with no trace of dampness around the three spots on one end . . . otherwise it will be rancid. To open the nut, hold it in one hand and hit it firmly with a hammer all around the centre, midway between the spots on one end and the point on the other. Keep turning the nut and tapping sharply until a crack appears. A couple more well placed taps and the nut should crack in two. Save the water – in a fresh nut it should be sweet and good for drinking.

In Asian countries and the Pacific Islands, so much fresh coconut is used that a coconut grater is standard equipment in every household. The easiest one to use screws onto a table top like a mincing machine. The grating is done by a number of curved, serrated metal blades that meet at a central point like a citrus juice extractor. The problem is that, with the western kitchen's built-in bench tops and glossy surfaces, there is nowhere to affix such a machine even if one could purchase it.

Other methods involve prising the coconut out of the shell with a pointed knife, which could be dangerous, and once you have it out you have to grate it on a conventional grater with the risk of skinned knuckles and broken nails.

Happily, now there is a hand-held coconut grater for the western kitchen. It is moulded in hard plastic, and fits into the half shell. It comes apart for easy storing in a drawer, is dishwasher proof and is a safe and easy way of grating coconut.

Pour 250 ml (8 fl oz) hot water over the grated flesh of half a medium-sized coconut, knead it firmly and squeeze out the milk through a strainer. Repeat a second and even a third time, adding more hot water.

If you don't have the grater described above, loosen the meat from the shell by placing the nut in a moderately low oven for 15 or 20 minutes, and when it starts to come away from the shell, lift it out with the point of a knife, exercising due care. Peel away the thin dark brown skin on the outside of the white meat. Cut the flesh into chunks and put it into an electric blender or food processor with 500 ml (18 fl oz) hot water and blend at high speed until the coconut is completely pulverised. Strain to extract all the milk. Repeat using the same coconut and more water.

Using dried coconut: Put 185 g (6½ oz) desiccated coconut into an electric blender, food processor or bowl and pour over 600 ml (1 pt) hot water. Cover and blend for 30 seconds on high speed. Strain through a fine sieve or double muslin, squeezing out as much moisture as possible. Repeat, using the same coconut and more hot water.

THINGS TO DO WHILE THE COALS ARE GLOWING

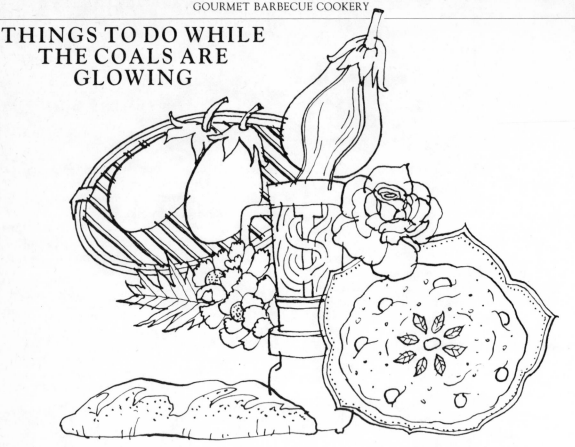

It always seems a pity to rake out those coals after the barbecue has finished. It takes a while to get them going, and I for one try not to waste them.

Here are a few things that are ideally done over coals but which, because time doesn't permit, are usually done in ovens and under grills. Think ahead and you can prepare a special dish for serving over the next day or two.

My first choice would be Baba Ghannouj. You've probably tasted it if you eat Middle Eastern food – it's a creamy, smoky, piquant dip based on aubergine (eggplant). The secret of the best Baba Ghannouj, though, is that the vegetable should be grilled over hot coals until it is cooked through. Just put it on the barbecue and leave it, because it does take quite some time for the skin to char and the flesh to soften. Turn with tongs until it has blackened all over.

Put the aubergines in a container and continue in the kitchen. It is much easier to remove the burned skin at the kitchen sink, using a trickle of cold water to rinse the clinging bits away. Another method is to split the vegetable in two and scoop out the flesh with a spoon, leaving the charred skin behind.

Put the pulp into a food processor or blender, and to each 250 g (9 oz) add 3 tbsp tahini (sesame paste), 2 garlic cloves crushed with 1 tsp salt, and 2 or 3 tbsp lemon juice.

Blend to a smooth purée. Serve as a dip with pitta bread or with raw or lightly blanched vegetables.

Another good use for those lingering coals is to cook large, red or green capsicums (peppers) over them. Once again, turn the capsicums (peppers) until they are blistered and scorched on all sides. Put them into a bag or wrap in a clean tea towel until cold. Remove the thin, transparent outer skin, and also the centre membrane and seeds. Slice the flesh into strips and dress with a little olive oil, a good grinding of sea salt and, if liked, a hint of crushed garlic. Serve as an accompaniment to other foods or as a first course with crusty bread.

Then, for the children, the last of the coals are just perfect for toasting marshmallows until they puff and turn golden. Of course they may be eaten as they are. But try them floated in a cup of hot chocolate which you've had the forethought to bring in a vacuum flask. Dessert and beverage in one.

INDEX